I Don't Believe That Either . . . However

I Don't Believe That Either
. . . However

Tucker E. Dawson Jr.

 CASCADE *Books* · Eugene, Oregon

Cascade Books
An Imprint of Wipf and Stock Publishers
199 W. 8th Ave., Suite 3
Eugene, OR 97401

www.wipfandstock.com

PAPERBACK ISBN: 978-1-6667-6530-4
HARDCOVER ISBN: 978-1-6667-6531-1
EBOOK ISBN: 978-1-6667-6532-8

Cataloguing-in-Publication data:

Names: Dawson, Tucker E., Jr.

Title: I don't believe that either . . . however / Tucker E. Dawson Jr.

Description: Eugene, OR: Cascade Books, 2024 | Includes bibliographical references.

Identifiers: ISBN 978-1-6667-6530-4 (paperback) | ISBN 978-1-6667-6531-1 (hardcover) | ISBN 978-1-6667-6532-8 (ebook)

Subjects: LCSH: Christianity—21st century. | Theology, Doctrinal—Popular works. | Liberalism (Religion).

Classification: BR124 .D40 2024 (print) | BR124 (ebook)

01/22/24

To Margene, my wife, and
Tucker, my son.

"Lord, I believe; help thou mine unbelief."

The Gospel According to Mark 9:24 KJV

Contents

Contents

Acknowledgments

I WISH TO EXPRESS my gratitude to those who helped me write this book. Doug Bristol was the first to press me into writing, and then proofread the manuscript chapter by chapter. My brother Doug Dawson also proofread every chapter, making helpful suggestions throughout. Al Eickelmann helped significantly by recommending Cascade Books. My onetime secretary, Wendy Nelson, by her skills at a computer, got me through many entanglements that could have derailed the project. My two neighbors did their part. The many discussions I had with Clay Andrews kept me thinking and probing. Skip Derry's questions drove me to go back and check myself on various points. Now, I must thank my wife, Margene, who put up with the many hours I abandoned her to writing, even when I got up in the middle of the night to follow up on an idea. These good people made it possible for me to bring the project to fruition, and I thank them.

Key to Translations of the Bible

GN   Good News
KJV   King James Version
NEB   New English Bible
NRSV   New Revised Standard Version
RSV   Revised Standard Version

Introduction

"I Don't Believe That Either" may seem a strange choice of title for someone who has been, for fifty years and more, an ordained clergyman. It is, though, precisely those years of experience that engendered the title.

A specific incident illustrates my point. A woman made an appointment with me, at which she explained that she was having trouble attending church because she could not in good conscience recite the Nicene Creed. Her problem, as I saw it, was that she had learned only one way to accept the creed, and that was to take it literally. I told her that I do not believe that either. Then I explained that in many places the Nicene Creed is metaphorical, expressing the faith in verbal images that are open to more than one interpretation. For example, "God from God, Light from Light, true God from true God" are phrases open to multiple interpretations. Following our discussion, she left much less troubled and continued to attend church.

This experience illustrates circumstances of a much broader range. However, the basic teaching of the church need not be rejected. There are optional understandings and explanations of many church doctrines seldom offered to the average church member. Among those options, some are found among traditional teachings and are supported by Holy Scripture. At one time in history, they could have been the primary expression of a belief or doctrine. My position is that these alternative options, often of ancient origin, are in various ways more compatible with our present-day scientific worldview. There is more than one way to skin a dogma. It is these other ways of understanding Christian beliefs that I will offer.

I do this because many adults in the Episcopal Church have no more than a simplistic, Sunday school understanding of Christianity. Their grasp of the faith is inadequate for coping with adult issues, such as the illness and death caused by COVID-19. I suspect this may be true as well in other denominations. In my consideration, these are some of the reasons the fastest growing "religious" group in the United States is the "Nones." I refer to those persons who, when asked their religious affiliation, declare that they have none. The number of Americans who consider themselves Christian is falling, according to several polls.

Some persons are outside the church, leaning toward becoming one of the "Nones," but hoping to find something more to life than competition and material acquisition. Some are in the church but struggling to stay there, trying to reconcile traditional church teachings with their sense of how the world works. Whether a "None" or a perplexed church member, one side of the problem is our present understanding of what makes the world go round. The understanding today, expressed succinctly, is that this is a world of matter and energy within time. We are educated into, even socialized into, a scientific worldview. We tend to think that this worldview leaves no room for any less materialistic alternatives. The side of this so-called conflict between science and religion that I feel competent to present is a Christianity that is not anti-intellectual, rigid, or defensive. There is a way of living, an explanation of beliefs, a reading of the Bible that can be ours without having to abandon our beliefs or our science.

An example of what I am offering is found in the alternative versions of the escape of the Israelites through the Red Sea. This is a significant event within the story of the exodus, the story of how Moses led the Israelites out of Egypt, through the wilderness, to the promised land. The older version, in the book of Exodus, is more naturalistic (Exod 14:21 NEB): "Then Moses stretched out his hand over the sea, and the Lord drove the sea away all night with a strong east wind and turned the sea-bed into dry land." Any who have been to the beach, and I live just three blocks from the beach on the Mississippi Gulf Coast, have observed that when the water recedes the sand becomes firm enough to drive a car on. The later version, which follows immediately upon the older, is much more supernatural (Exod 14:22 NEB): "The waters were torn apart, and the Israelites went through the sea on dry ground, while the waters made a wall for them to right and to left." The later version is distinctly miraculous and dramatic, and quite more memorable even without the visual impact provided by the 1956 movie *The Ten Commandments*.

My point is that it is no less Christian, or religious, or faithful to accept the more naturalistic version. It is undoubtedly closer to the truth, and more reasonable. It is not necessary to faith that we give assent to the supernatural version of this event, or to any other event, and then defend it as factual or historical. Today that approach is detrimental to an acceptance of the Christian faith.

Within the teachings of the church there are acceptable theological positions that are not incompatible with our modern worldview. There are optional explanations, as I would call them, some of which have been around for years, some of which, like the biblical story of the Exodus, can be found in the original telling of the story. Though some of the options are less well known, they are nonetheless acceptable and valid. Often, these options are found by approaching from down here where we are, with an immanent God, rather than from up there, with a transcendent God. For further discussion of this approach see the Sidebar following this Introduction.

Through the years, I have adopted some of these optional positions because I do not believe Christianity is as much a matter of correct beliefs and good behavior as it is a matter of relationships. I do not believe God wrote the Bible, or in any way dictated it to puppetlike authors. I do not believe Jesus knew every detail of his future, as if he had already seen every episode of the drama. I do not believe the church is called to be a border patrol for the sacraments or a police force for morals. I have become comfortable in responding to individuals and in classes and discussions with the five words, "I don't believe that either!" Those few words often provided a gambit that helped lead the conversation or discussion into a wider range of possibilities for teaching and learning.

My interest in teaching has always been evident. I received a BS in education from Louisiana State University in Baton Rouge, and then, following a short time on active duty with the National Guard, I taught for a year in the public school system of Ascension Parish in Louisiana. I then entered the school of theology at the University of the South, in Sewanee, Tennessee. My background in education led to my first position following graduation from seminary. I became the head of school at St. Paul's Episcopal School in New Orleans, and assistant to the priest of St. Paul's Church. During my seven years at St. Paul's, I earned a MEd in administration and supervision at what is now the University of New Orleans.

Toward the end of those years, I decided that my calling was to pastoral ministry rather than school administration. In thirty-six years of ministry, serving three churches as rector following my time at St. Paul's, I made

Christian education for adults one of my priorities. I held it as a priority after retirement as I served five churches, two of them a second time, as interim rector. Serving as an interim, between two full-time rectors, is very satisfying. In most cases, an interim is not expected to get involved in the day-to-day management of the parish church. This allows for full attention to be given to central aspects of ministry: pastoral care, leading worship, preaching, and teaching. My experiences over those forty-plus years of ministry motivated me to investigate my own beliefs and to write them out with coherence and clarity for myself and for those I hope may read this final foray into teaching.

The organization of the material into short chapters is by design, as is the overall length of the book. It is meant to be short enough that a person would see it as a book to be read over a weekend, in a couple of days. Also, providing more full quotations from the Bible is for the reader's convenience, particularly for the reader without a Bible and with little knowledge of the Bible. I have used numerous translations to demonstrate that there is no one verbally perfect English translation. Each translation has been selected according to how clearly it supports the point I am making. (See the Key to Translations of the Bible.) Concerning the Sidebars, I chose to use them to elaborate a concept or bit of information that I found of interest and importance. And, though I consider the information in each Sidebar to be related to the subject of the chapter it follows, I think that if it were included within the chapter, it would be an interruption or distraction. Also, having such information in a Sidebar makes it more accessible. It seems to me better to include these additional concepts and associated items of interest in Sidebars.

Declaring "I don't believe that either" is my way of breaking out of traditional teachings into other options. Here are two fundamentals that have guided me. Beginning down here, with an immanent God, rather than up there, with a transcendent God, is my approach. Christianity as relationships is my leading principle.

In the following chapters I will endeavor to present alternative ways to understand the teachings of the church that I think are more acceptable in our scientifically driven world than what we are led to believe are the only, and inflexible, beliefs to be held by Christians. This, I trust, will appeal to the questioning Christian and to the hopeful "None," helping each to find a more fulfilling life. We need not abandon either faith or science.

SIDEBAR

My Approach

I PROVIDE HERE A brief explanation of the approach I take when studying the church's teachings. God is said to be "transcendent," up there, beyond this world in which we live. God is also said to be "immanent," down here, actively present in our world. It seems to me that many of the beliefs of Christianity are explained by approaching them "from above," beginning with a transcendent God. I will endeavor to approach them "from below," beginning with an immanent God.

Beginning "from above" requires various amounts of speculation. We must suppose some things to be so before we can get underway. Beginning here, within our own experiences, adopting more naturalistic interpretations, should make Christianity more accessible. So, in my estimation, the place to begin when investigating things Christian is "down here" rather than "up there."

Take as an example the church's doctrine of the divinity of Jesus. It was not heralded from above at the outset of Jesus' ministry. Setting the Christmas stories aside, for they fall into a different category, and following the story of Jesus and his disciples, we find that the disciples' awareness of who Jesus was developed over time. Though a short history, he and they had a history. First, he was their teacher. Then he was thought to be the Messiah. Only later was he considered to be the Son of God. It was not until the early Christians realized they were thinking of Jesus in much the same terms they had customarily reserved for God that they began to speak of his divinity. This became an issue. And, it was not until the first quarter of the fourth century, at the Council of Nicaea, that the divinity of Jesus, and his humanity, were formally expressed. The creedal formula came at the end of a lengthy process, worked out by real people, right down here in this real world.

As I tried to explain to the woman who came to me with her trouble reciting the creed, it is our product, a human product, and therefore open to our use, reinterpretations, and even revision, as we try to put our beliefs into words. This is true not only of the creed, but also of many ways we define and express the Christian faith.

And so, rather than begin with the transcendent God who is beyond us, I like to begin with the immanent God who is with us, and with whom we have a history. This approach will lead us to helpful alternative explanations and understandings of Christian beliefs. My hope is that we will come to a place where we need not give up either on common sense or on God. I am indebted to Wolfhart Pannenberg, who approached Christology "from below," thereby reinforcing my decision to begin "from below" in considering all things Christian.[1]

1. Pannenberg, *Jesus—God and Man*, 33.

PART I

Relationships

I

Beliefs and Behavior

I DON'T BELIEVE CHRISTIANITY is a matter of correct beliefs or good behavior. Christianity is a matter of relationships, and relationships matter. Of what importance, then, are our beliefs or our behavior? They have their place, second place; they are the result of our relationships rather than their cause.

Beliefs have become little more than opinions. Beliefs are considered to be thoughts. They are mental constructs that take place in our heads. Within Christianity, belief has become assent to a list of mental constructs we hold without facts to support them, many of which now seem unbelievable. For instance, a boat that can hold two of every living creature. Correct belief is not what Christianity is all about. Christianity is of the heart, not just the head. I like this passage: "the devils also believe, and tremble" (Jas 2:19b KJV). It says, in a way, that it is possible to believe and still be a mess. Affirmation of facts is not faith. Faith is trust, trust in a relationship, trust in a person.

Good behavior is too often used as a bargaining chip. "God, this is what I will do for you. I will go to Mass every day, I will not dance or drink, I will not cheat. Then, God, I will expect you to do this or that for me." We turn Christianity into a transaction. The mistake is that grace is a gift, not a reward. Grace is God's gift to us of himself, not something we earn by our behavior. Our relationship with God is an accomplished fact, already ours, subject only to our acceptance. There is no need or place for a transaction. Also, Christianity as good behavior segues into a morality that catalogues rights and wrongs without consideration of the ambiguous nature of life. Moral behavior must become more than obeying a list of rules, rules we often break even as we fight over which to accept and which to reject. The rules of the various churches concerning marriage, divorce, annulment, and remarriage are a good illustration. In the heat of a wedding, little thought is given to having and holding "from this day forward, for better for worse, for richer or poorer, in sickness and in health, to love and to cherish, until we are parted by death."[1] This "solemn vow," found on page 427 in *The Book of Common Prayer*, Episcopal Church, USA, gets buried under church rules and wedding costs.

Historically, Christianity as beliefs and behavior led to horrible behavior as Christians inflicted terrible cruelties on other Christians because they held different beliefs. It won't do. The historic creeds we recite in church make matters worse. Because of changes in the meaning of words, as soon as we say, "I believe," or "We believe," we are off on the wrong foot. When we use the word "believe" in a creed we are not giving intellectual assent to what follows. The word "creed" has a much deeper meaning: "I give my heart to," "I put my trust in." "I bet my life on" what I am saying.

Trusting someone, betting your life on another person, is to move into a relationship with that person. While writing this, those first old Tarzan movies were on TV. Watching them led me to think about the Tarzan fable, which is just that, a fable. In 1912, the American author Edgar Rice Burroughs wrote *Tarzan of the Apes*. As the story begins, a British lord and lady and their infant son are marooned on the Atlantic coast of Africa. Following the deaths of his parents, this infant boy is adopted and raised by apes. This boy, who is named Tarzan, grows up without any flaws of character. As a man, he is ethical, generous, affectionate, gracious, and noble. Tarzan is the perfect human being, not despite being raised by apes in the jungle, but because of that upbringing. The story of Tarzan is a classic example of the "back to nature" theme in literature. The point being made by calling this story a fable is that humans must be nurtured by humans into becoming humans.

Apes can raise only more apes. It is through personal relationships that we have any hope of becoming persons. Human beings are designed to find themselves in their relationships with other selves. Without any relationship of love and trust our emotional and physical development is stunted and warped. No person is self-sufficient, and the myth of the rugged individual, though a formative American myth, is still only a myth. All

---

1. Episcopal Church, *Book of Common Prayer*, 427.

of us are embedded in family, friends, community, laws, and customs, and just as surely indebted to numerous people within those institutions.

We are created for community, for one another, and few of us do well in isolation. That is why using a "time out" to discipline a child will, in most instances, be effective. In case you do not know, a "time out" is executed by removing the offending child from the company of those other children he or she has been tormenting. He or she is placed in isolation for whatever is deemed to be an appropriate length of time. The punishment is separation from the community. Much the same punishment is inflicted on offending adults. They are incarcerated, separated from the community. When deemed necessary they are put in isolation, which is considered an extreme form of punishment, and so it is. We need one another. We need companionship. Good relationships are necessary for a good life.

I was fortunate to have a good relationship with my father. He seemed to understand that I hated school beyond anything else in my life, and that my attitude toward Sunday school was no different. The consequences of that relationship were long lasting. At about the age of twelve I was presented to the bishop for confirmation, which took place in Trinity Episcopal Church, just a few doors down from my home in Baton Rouge, Louisiana. Soon after my confirmation, the rector of the parish asked if I would like to become an acolyte. I decided to try to cut a deal. I offered to serve as an acolyte, regularly and faithfully, if I could be permanently excused from Sunday school. I succeeded. From that time, on many a Sunday, I walked with my father to a service in that Trinity Church. He would take his place in the congregation, and I would take mine at the altar. Those years of serving at the altar are part of what led me to attend seminary and become an Episcopal priest. The irony of the deal I made is that in escaping a few short Sunday school classes I condemned myself to three additional years of demanding education beyond college. At the time that I attended seminary, a master of divinity degree required three years of study, maintaining a B average, and doing all required New Testament studies in Greek. My life in ministry, to a significant degree, was the consequence of the relationship between me, my father, and the rector of Trinity Church, Stratton Lawrence. The result was much to my benefit. Life is a matrix of relationships and their influences. I quote Robin R. Meyers, from his book *Saving Jesus from the Church*: "We are as we relate."[2]

2. Meyers, *Saving Jesus from the Church*, 203.

Part I: Relationships

For those who require biblical support for understanding Christianity as a matter of relationships, something over and above my personal experience, these observations are offered. To begin, in all our relationships with God he is the one who takes the initiative. This is a biblical truth. The Bible is the story of a relationship given, lost, and offered back again and again. I can touch only the high points of this long story. We are given a life in relationship to God that is described as being with God: "walking in the garden at the time of the evening breeze" (Gen 3:8 NEB). We soon scuttled that. How we managed to do the scuttling is a subject for later consideration. It's enough, now, to point out that from the end of chapter 3 of the book of Genesis to the last word in the book of Revelation, the Bible is an account of God's many attempts to reestablish his relationship with us, attempts at reconciliation. The positive aspect is that we cannot totally destroy the relationship because God never gives up on us.

Evidence of God's initiative is found throughout the early prehistory of the Hebrew people. God chose Abram, who would soon become known as Abraham, promising him that he would be blessed and would become a blessing to all people: "The Lord said to Abram, 'Leave your own country, your kinsmen, and your father's house, and go to a country that I will show you. I will make you into a great nation, I will bless you and make your name so great that it shall be used in blessings: Those that bless you I will bless, those that curse you, I will execrate. All the families on earth will pray to be blessed as you are blessed'" (Gen 12:1–3 NEB). This covenant motif is repeated again and again, and in even more specific terms: "I make this covenant, and I make it with you: you shall be the father of a host of nations. Your name shall no longer be Abram, your name shall be Abraham, for I make you father of a host of nations. . . . I will fulfill my covenant between myself and you and your descendants after you . . . to be your God" (Gen 17:4–7 NEB). A covenant was established, and whatever else a covenant may be, it is an agreement that establishes a relationship. Found here is the earliest account of God taking the initiative to mend the relationship that had been broken. The nature of this broken relationship, and its consequences, will be taken up in chapter 3. We Christians believe even now that we are living in that damaged relationship, with the God of Abraham as our God and we as his people.

Moving ahead again, God selected Moses to orchestrate the release of the Hebrew people from their slavery in Egypt. "Moses was minding the flock of his father-in-law Jethro, the priest of Midian. He led the flock along the side of the wilderness and came to Horeb, the mountain of God. There the angel of the Lord appeared to him in the flame of a burning bush . . . it was not being burned up. . . . When the Lord saw that Moses had turned aside to look, he called to him out of the bush, 'Moses, Moses'" (Exod 3:1–4 NEB). "Come now; I will send you to Pharaoh and you shall bring my people Israel out of Egypt" (Exod 3:10 NEB). In the course of the Israelites' escape a covenant code was established. The earliest and most well-known part of that code is the Decalogue, the Ten Commandments, that are found in two places, Exodus 20:1–17 and Deuteronomy 5:1–21.

Here is a summary of the Ten Commandments from the perspective that they can be interpreted as guidance for our relationships. The first four cover our relationship with God: 1- have no other gods; 2- make no idols; 3- don't use God's name for evil intent; 4- observe the Sabbath. The final six cover our relationships with one another: 5- honor your parents; 6- don't commit murder; 7- don't commit adultery; 8- don't steal; 9- don't lie; 10- don't covet. The Ten Commandments guide our relationship with God and our relationships with one another.

We pretend to observe the Ten Commandments as hard-and-fast laws, but we actually do no such thing. At a very early date in its history, the church altered its observance of commandment number four, replacing the Sabbath with Sunday as the day they would "keep holy." In the case of number five, "Honor your father and your mother," we recognize that some parents are too abusive or neglectful to deserve being honored, and we excuse breaking this commandment. When we come to number six, "You shall not commit murder," we become sticklers for the letter of the law, which is a reverse of our attitude toward the other commandments. We are opposed to murder, but in some circumstances, we allow and even approve of killing. We execute criminals and engage in what we call "just" wars. Without acknowledging it, as we take the circumstances, the situation, into consideration, we adopt "situation ethics." In situation ethics, an act is evaluated within the surrounding circumstances that influenced it.

It is also important to recognize that, according to the Gospel record, Jesus never made direct reference to the Ten Commandments. They are, with the exception of number five, negative decrees that begin, "Thou shalt not . . ." Jesus replaced them with one positive commandment in two parts. This "summary of the Law" is found in Mark's Gospel. "Then one of the lawyers, who had been listening to these discussions and had noted how well he answered, came forward and asked him, 'Which commandment is first of all?' Jesus answered, 'The first is, "Hear, O Israel: The Lord our God is the only Lord; love the Lord your god with all your heart, with all your soul, with all your mind, and with all your strength." The second is this: "Love your neighbour as yourself." There is no other commandment greater than these"' (Mark 12:28–31 NEB). Love is certainly a relationship. For his "Great Commandment" Jesus turned to two passages, Deuteronomy 6:4–5 and Leviticus 19:18. He did not turn to the Ten Commandments.

Moving on from these observations on the Ten Commandments, consider next the prophets of the Old Testament. They fit in here as they endeavored, each in his own way, to get Israel to be faithful to the covenant. The words of the prophet Jeremiah offer something of a bridge between the prophets and Jesus: "The time is coming, says the Lord, when I will make a new covenant with Israel and Judah" (Jer 31:31 NEB). " I will set my law within them and write it on their hearts; I will become their God and they shall become my people" (Jer 31:33b NEB). External rules are to be replaced by internal motivation.

The life of Jesus is next on the agenda. However the life and work of Jesus is interpreted (a topic for later), the life and death of Jesus is God's most audacious initiative to heal the rent in our relationships with himself and with one another. The kingdom of God was at the heart of Jesus' message, and the kingdom of God can be understood as right relationships all around. Jesus' inaugural address, as it has been called, is recorded in Mark's Gospel: "Now after John (the Baptist) was arrested, Jesus came to Galilee proclaiming the good news of God, and saying, 'The time is fulfilled, and the kingdom of God has come near; repent, and believe in the good news.'" (Mark 1:14–15 NRSV). Jesus is responsible for the relationship we have with God.

St. Paul provides the right words for bringing this biblical review to a conclusion: "From first to last this has been the work of God. He has reconciled us men to himself through Christ, and he has enlisted us in this service of reconciliation. What I mean is, that God was in Christ reconciling the world to himself, no longer holding men's misdeeds against them, and that he has entrusted us with the message of reconciliation" (2 Cor 5:18–19 NEB). *Reconciliation* is a relationship word, and the initiative is God's. In the sense that salvation may be considered as being led home, of finding our way to the essence of life, which is life in loving relationships, reconciliation is a practical synonym for salvation.

All of the above is brought down to earth in Jesus' parable of the nations (Matt 25:31–46 GN). "And the King will answer them, 'Truly I tell you just as you did it to one of the least important of these followers of mine, you did it to me'" (Matt 25:40). The same point is made, in the reverse, as what we do not do (Matt 25:45). One meaning that can be found in the parable is that we work out and live into our relationship with God among each other right here on this earth. As God is constantly taking the initiative to draw us into a better relationship with himself, others become involved. This is so because all our relationships with one another and with God are intertwined. Our relationship with God is the basis for our relationships with one another. And, how we relate to one another informs and cultivates our relationship with God.

The Bible is about relationships, our relationships now with God and one another. Our relationship with God is not some pie-in-the-sky spirituality, but an earthy way of living with and loving those around us. It is from down here, with one another, that we move up into our relationship with God. Relationships matter, and Christianity is a matter of relationships.

SIDEBAR

Words of Belief

THE LANGUAGE OF EARLY Christian documents is Latin. In Latin, the word for "belief" is *opinionem*, the root of our English word "opinion." The creed is more than an opinion. The Latin word *credo*, from which we get our word "creed," means "I give my loyalty to."

Credo was translated "belief" in medieval English, and at that time it meant roughly the same thing as the German word *belieben*. *Belieben* means "to hold dear." The connection is the German for "love," which is *lieb*. To "believe" was to "belove," to treasure and to trust. When we recite one of the Christian creeds, we are expressing more than an opinion. We are saying "We bet our life on this." We stake our life on this being true. We would more appropriately begin the Christian creeds with the words, "We trust."[1]

Just one caveat: we cannot take the words of any of the creeds literally. We can, though, take them faithfully. The creeds are full of figures of speech, metaphors, and similes: "Light from Light," "at the right hand of the Father." These images make the creeds broad and rich in meaning. When reciting one of the creeds we are using words in the best way we can to express the truth of our faith. As we stretch our language to express what we cannot fully understand, in a rich use of images, we are saying much more than the literal meaning of the words. In the creeds we are saying even more than we may think we are saying.

1. Bass, *Christianity after Religion*, 117.

2

Inside and Outside

I DON'T BELIEVE EVIL is outside us trying to get in. I do believe there is evil inside us trying to get out and succeeding. It is helpful to begin by making a distinction between "evil" and "bad."

With the word "bad" I refer to natural disturbances and calamities: hurricanes, tornadoes, earthquakes, and accidents. Illness should be included in this list, along with fire, flood, and pestilence. All are very bad, but none are evil. The distinction is that bad things are the consequences of natural developments while evil is the consequence of choice. There must be willful intent to do harm for there to be evil. Evil is the result of a free agent, a person, willfully misusing that freedom to the detriment of another.

I offer an illustration. If you are walking through the woods, and due to natural aging, weather, and rot, a limb falls and smacks you on the head, that is bad. If I break a limb loose, or pick it up, lay in wait until you walk by, and smack you on the head with it, that is evil. I made a willful decision, for whatever reason, to do you harm. Our freedom to act in such a way will be considered later.

The disturbing thing is that we smack one another much too frequently. Evil is pervasive, systemic, human. Even when bad things are separated out there is a lot of hurt in the world, enough that we are not altogether wrong to personify evil and name it Satan, the devil. It is a serious mistake, though, to imagine Satan to be an actual creature rather than an image of our fabrication. It is even worse to ascribe the attributes of God to this mythical creature. Satan, the devil, is not all-knowing, present everywhere, or all-powerful. When we think in those terms, we are envisioning a second sort of god.

There are several loosely related issues to be considered in an examination of the reality of Satan. First, we need to turn back to the creation story in the book of Genesis: "God said, 'Let there be light,' and there was light; and God saw that the light was good, and he separated light from darkness" (Gen 1:3–4 NEB). God's declaration that all is good covers his act of creation from beginning to end. In the final verse of Genesis chapter one, God creates all living creatures, human beings included, and pronounces all to be good. "So it was; and God saw all that he had made, and it was very good. Evening came, and morning came, a sixth day" (Gen 1:31 NEB). Creation is good, life is good, and this attitude is presented in the creation myth as God's doing. Evil, in this portrayal of creation, is an absence of good. It is a negative. Evil does not exist in and of itself. It is the absence of good. There is no ontological evil. This means that there is no actual evil creature of any name, Satan, the devil, Beelzebub.

Second, creation is an ongoing, dynamic process. This means that the act of creation should not be thought of in the past tense. Creation does not exist because God made it, but because God is continually making it. Life is constantly pouring into the world. As creation moves forward, things that at one time existed are no more; and things now exist that did not before. A passage of Holy Scripture that supports the concept of an ongoing, continuing creation is found in John's Gospel. Jesus is accused of breaking the law by healing and by working on the Sabbath. "He defended himself by saying, 'My Father has never yet ceased to work, and I am working too'" (John 5:17 NEB). If Satan exists as more than a mythical creature, he is a creation of God, and his existence is sustained by God. I find it very difficult to believe that a good and loving God would allow an evil creature to disrupt his creation, to prey upon it, when the extinction of that creature would not require that God do anything. It is not what God would do, but simply what he would stop doing. God would need only to withdraw his creative, life-giving support, and that would be the end of Satan. I cannot fit Satan into an understanding of creation as a dynamic, ongoing process, orchestrated by a loving God.

There is, though, a dualism found in the Bible, in the Old Testament and in the New. It is due to the influence of Zoroastrianism. Zoroaster taught that all creation was involved in a conflict between good and bad, light and dark. In Zoroastrian doctrine there is an Evil Spirit in mortal combat with a Good God. This is an ancient mythology the Hebrew people were exposed to as they were conquered by neighboring powers. This dualistic belief was influenced further by Greek thought, which resulted in that Evil Spirit being identified as the devil. The Greek word for devil is *diabolos*, from which we get our words "diabolic" and "diabolical" (see Sidebar).

Third, among the myths regarding Satan he is identified as a fallen angel. There are only two references to fallen angels in the New Testament. "God did not spare the angels who sinned but consigned them to the dark pits of Hell" (2 Pet 2:4 NEB). According to tradition, St. Peter was martyred in Rome during the persecution of Christians by Nero in 64 CE. It should be noted that this letter is dated at around 100, possibly later, and could not have been written by St. Peter. I regard this passage as a flight of pure mythology by an unknown author. The other reference is, "He replied, 'I watched how Satan fell, like lightening out of the sky'" (Luke 10:18 NEB). I regard this an example of Jesus using a strong and positive image to praise his disciples. The seventy-two whom Jesus had sent out on a mission had returned and Jesus was commending them. I am aware that this passage is interpreted as being related to the book of Isaiah: "How you have fallen from heaven, bright morning star, felled to earth, sprawling helpless across the nations!" (Isa 14:12 NEB). St. Jerome, in the Vulgate Bible, translated the Hebrew for "bright morning star" as "Lucifer," (light-bearer in Latin). The actual reference in Isaiah is to the "king of Babylon" (Isa 14:4). The reference here is to a king who has fallen, not to a fallen angel, and not to Satan. Jesus, I suspect, was speaking figuratively.

Fourth, consideration must also be given to the accounts of the temptations of Jesus found in the Gospels of Matthew, Mark, and Luke. I begin with the account of the temptation found in Mark's Gospel because it is the earliest account and the most succinct. "Thereupon the Spirit sent him away into the wilderness, and there he remained for forty days tempted by Satan. He was among the wild beasts; and angels waited on him" (Mark 1:12–13 NEB). The accounts in the Gospels of Matthew and Luke expand upon Mark's brief account of the temptations. The stories in Matthew and Luke are almost identical; the major difference is a change in the sequence of the temptations. Each tell of three specific temptations and give Jesus' response. In Matthew's Gospel (Matt 4:2–11), Jesus is tempted: 1) to appease his hunger by turning stones into bread; 2) to wow the people by jumping from the parapet of the temple without sustaining any injury, and

3) to rule all the kingdoms of the world. In Luke's Gospel, the second and third temptations are reversed (Luke 4:1–13). These two accounts, with the same three temptations, are very stylized. It appears they were composed for easy memorization. In the nonliterate culture of the time, a construction of the temptations of Jesus in a form that could be easily memorized was important. These accounts of the temptations are obviously mystical in nature, even supernatural.

John's Gospel, in contrast, does not have a short, stylized version of the temptations. This Gospel provides us with a more natural account of how Jesus was tempted. If Jesus were genuinely human, he would have encountered temptations throughout his life. It would not have been "three strikes and you're out" for Satan. In this Gospel we find that Jesus is tempted much more in the way we are. In the Gospel according to John, it reads: "'They said, 'What sign can you give us to see, so that we may believe you? What is the work you do? Our ancestors had manna to eat in the desert; as Scripture says, 'He gave them bread from heaven to eat'" (John 6:30–31 NEB). They want a sign, but Jesus does not, at this time, miraculously provide bread for them. Then, his brothers said, "You should leave this district and go into Judaea, so that your disciples there may see the great things you are doing. Surely no one can hope to be in the public eye if he works in seclusion" (John 7:3–4 NEB). Get out of the backwoods, they are saying to him, go to where the people are, to the cities of Judaea, and wow them. He refuses. Also, "Jesus, aware that they meant to come and seize him to proclaim him king, withdrew again to the hills by himself" (John 6:15 NEB). Jesus would have none of it. I subscribe to John's version of the temptations, not because the others are untrue, but because I believe the less supernatural version, without any reference to Satan, is more in keeping with Jesus being an actual and genuine person. The Gospels teach that Jesus was tempted just as we are. For Jesus to be tempted as we are there is no need to drag the devil into the picture.

I have an illustration that is rather dated. Some, though, will remember *The Flip Wilson Show* that was on TV in the mid-1970s. It was a very popular show, and a highlight of each episode was a skit in which the comedian, Flip Wilson, came out in wig, dress and lipstick, as Geraldine Jones, one of his comic characters. Geraldine was always into some mischief. When she got caught, as always happened, she would say, "The devil made me do it." The TV audience recognized this as a blatant excuse, and it always got a laugh. Quite possibly it was a nervous laugh, because we all knew

Geraldine was doing just what we often do when caught red-handed. We try to shift the blame. Shifting the blame onto a mythical personification of evil makes sense only if we adopt a nonnatural, metaphysical understanding of creation.

If we say there is no Satan, the next question is, what about hell? If there is no Satan, as an evil ruling creature, is there then no evil realm, no hell? If Satan is not an actual creature, is hell an actual place? The first thing to say in response to this question is that we should not ascribe time and space to hell, or to heaven. It is very difficult, of course, for us to imagine ourselves outside of time and space. However, to think of heaven and hell in space-time categories is to be faced with the unanswerable question: "Where?" To get around this impossible question, heaven and hell may each be thought of in terms of relations. Eternal life, then, is not considered existence through every moment of future time, in some place, but as being independent of both space and time. It may even be considered a continuation of the relationships we begin to develop here in this life.

Going back to the Hebrew people at the time of Jesus, the Sadducees thought of death as total extinction. For the Pharisees, the dead continued to exist, but in a sort of half-life in a region of shadows. This region was *Sheol* in Hebrew and *Hades* in Greek. Eventually, this region was called "hell." The image for hell was *Gehenna*, the Valley of Hinnom, the city dump outside Jerusalem where garbage continually burned, and smoked, and stunk. A good image for a bad place.

One of the strongest, and most Christian images of heaven and hell that I have come across is by C. S. Lewis. What first caught my attention is that those in hell could take a bus tour through heaven. And they could get off the bus and stay in heaven if they wished.[1] Most, though, chose to make it a round trip. What they returned to was a gray and lonely existence in which people were forever moving farther apart, isolating themselves, bringing all relationships to an end. The description in C. S. Lewis's story of an accessible heaven at one end of the bus trip and a dreary hell at the other, though spatial images, open the way to an alternative image already mentioned. Heaven and hell can be thought of in the language of relationships. We can then think in terms of a continuum, with a perfect relationship with God and all others at one end, and no relationships whatsoever at the other. Life may be heavenly, or it may be hellish. Whichever we choose, the pattern begins to form in our relationships right here and now. When

1. Lewis, *Great Divorce*, 22.

we choose, or turn, one way or the other, it is our doing. God's invitation to join him is constant.

God is constant in his love for his creation, or so the New Testament would have us believe. There is no evil power or creature "out there" trying to lead us astray, trying to destroy our relationships with God and one another, trying to bring us to a bad end. Any bad end is of our own choosing. This is expressed in the adage "he has become his own worst enemy." When it comes to wrecking our relationships, we are often our own worst enemy. The real dualism in Christianity is not a mythical battle between the powers of light and dark. It is the strain, the tug of war, between God's will and our willfulness. In my opinion, that is what C. S. Lewis is saying when he writes, "There are only two kinds of people in the end: those who say to God 'Thy will be done,' and those to whom God says, in the end, '*thy* will be done.'"[2] The relationship is between us and God, without outside interference, except, perhaps, for all those other persons around us.

2. Lewis, *Great Divorce*, 75.

SIDEBAR

The Adversary

OUR WORD "SATAN" IN the Hebrew language means nothing more than "adversary." In the Old Testament it is used of ordinary human adversaries. The angel of the Lord is the satan who stands in Balaam's way (Num 22:22). The Philistines fear that David may become their satan (1 Sam 19:22). Solomon declares that God has given him such peace and prosperity that he has no satan left to oppose him (1 Kgs 5:4). In each of these examples, the word "satan" refers only to an adversary, and nothing more sinister. The word began by meaning adversary in the simplest sense.[1]

Subsequently, the word "satan" began to mean "one who pleads a case against a person." It is in this sense that the word is used in the first chapter of the book of Job. In that chapter, Satan (now capitalized) is no less than one of the sons of God (Job 1:6). His task is to consider men (Job 1:7) and to search for some case against them that could be pleaded before God. The word is also used in this way in the book of Zechariah (Zech 3:2). The task of Satan was to find anything that could be said against a person. He was now the accuser of men before God.

The other title for Satan is the devil. The word "devil" comes from the Greek word *diabolos*, which literally means "slanderer." It is a small step from one who accuses a person before God, perhaps rightfully so, to one who will deliberately and maliciously slander that person. The devil will

1. Barclay, *Gospel of Mark*, 24.

accuse man and even slander him before God. Satan, the devil, is the adversary of man. Even so, Satan is an emissary of God and not yet the malignant and supreme enemy of God.

There is then another step in the understanding of Satan. The Jewish people were subjects of Persia for 207 years, from 539 to 332 BCE. Through this time of subjugation, they were influenced by the Persians. Persian thought is dualistic, based on the conception that in the universe there are two powers, a power of good and a power of evil, of light and of dark, Ormuzd and Ahriman, respectively. The entire universe is a battleground between them, and man must choose a side in the conflict. Under Persian influence, Satan became "the adversary par excellence," God's adversary. Step by step, through the years, there was a transition in the meaning of the word from "satan," "adversary," to Satan the malignant adversary of God.[2] Satan is now the name of a mythical evil being, an opponent of God, destructive to creation and a great danger to all humans. A mythical being can pose no threat!

2. Barclay, *Gospel of Mark*, 25.

3

Sin and sins

I DON'T BELIEVE SINS are the problem. To explain, a distinction must be made between "Sin," with a capital "S" and in the singular, and "sins," with a small "s" and in the plural.

I use the word "Sin" for the evil that is in us, internal, a component of human nature. In this usage of the word, it designates a systemic disorder, a malady. We have a desire, a need, to be at the center of our world. We want all around us to treat us as special and bow to our wishes. We are egocentric creatures. No matter how strongly we deny that this is so, in our more honest moments we know it to be true. Sin is a self-serving disorder that motivates us to do whatever we can to have our own way, to overreach. It alienates us from one another, doing serious harm to our relationships all around us. When we push ourselves into the center, we push others out. From the Christian perspective, we push God out as well, usurping his rightful place and disrupting any relationship we have with him.

I use the word "sins" for those specific acts, or failures to act, that harm or hurt another person. By these behaviors we alienate ourselves from one another. To bring Christian teaching in again, what we do to alienate ourselves from another person also alienates us from God. To support this assertion, I turn to Matthew's Gospel. "I tell you this: anything you did for one of my brothers here, however humble, you did for me" (Matt 25:40 NEB). And the reverse: "I tell you this: anything you did not do for one of these, however humble, you did not do for me" (Matt 25:45 NEB). What we do, or fail to do, our actions and inactions, when harmful, are sins.

To illustrate the distinction between Sin and sins, I use chicken pox as an analogy. Like chicken pox, Sin is the malady that infects us. Like the rash, the red bumps, sins are a symptom of the malady. As applying lotion to the red bumps gives only limited relief, focusing on the sins is only a partial remedy. Attention to the malady is the best, if not the only, remedy. It is important that our primary attention be given to the affliction, the Sin.

As a teenager growing up in Baton Rouge in the early 1950s, I witnessed what I have come to regard as a misguided focus on "sins." I went to a small high school on the LSU campus, University High. There were only forty-one students in my graduating class, as I recall, and several of us had been together through the elementary grades in the University Laboratory School. We were a fairly close-knit group. Most of our parties throughout our high school years included dancing to recorded music. Our refreshments were seldom more than Coca-Cola. Because of the dancing, the parents of one classmate did not allow their daughter to attend any of the parties. I have wondered how she felt, being separated from her classmates when they were having fun together. And I now think that the limitation of her relationships with us, brought about by her restrictive parents, was far more sinful than a few dances.

One additional and more current observation, related to the example above, is that we hear great disapproval of sex, though it is a natural biological drive, and not necessarily evil. At the same time, we hear little disapproval of violence, which should be unnatural and is always evil. This disparity is particularly obvious in TV crime dramas. They grow progressively more violent and there is little or no protest, with few restrictions imposed.

The sins we commit cannot be easily excused or lightly forgiven. They injure others. They are harmful to the fabric of life. They are destructive to our relationships. Even so, Sin is the basic origin of the problem. Though it is not within my purview to consider why we are sinful creatures, I think this very human condition is caused by our awareness of our mortality. Our push to the center, our climb to the top, our need to be above all others, is a reach for security in an ambiguous and risky world. Sin is our way, though not a particularly successful way, of coping with the inevitability of death.

There are two challenges to our ability to cope with Sin. The first is our doubt that God will adequately cope with Sin. Our doubt becomes obvious when we look, even superficially, at what we do to stamp out anything we believe to be sinful. There was the Inquisition of the thirteenth century, which lasted, in one form or another, into the nineteenth century. During the early years of the Inquisition, those considered sinful heretics were hunted down and sentenced to severe and cruel executions. During the Reformation, which began in the sixteenth century, and is still with us, Catholics and Protestants defamed each other when they were not killing each other, all to protect the church from Sin. Today, in the twenty-first century, in what is considered a more humane society, those suspected of being sinners are ostracized, shunned, and cast out of our churches.

I remember the pastor of a large congregation who claimed that there were no alcoholics in his church—a bold claim considering the percentage of alcoholics in the general population. I challenged him. His response was that those members of his congregation suspected of drinking alcohol were told to stop or leave the church. God is not tough enough on Sin, he seemed to say, so we must be. And there shall be no dancing.

How we might better approach Sin and sinners is highlighted in the parable of the wheat and the weeds: "A man sowed good seed in his field. One night, when everyone was asleep, an enemy came and sowed weeds among the wheat and went away. When the plants grew and the heads of grain began to form, the weeds showed up. The man's servants came to him and said . . . 'Do you want us to go and pull up the weeds?' They were told, 'Let the wheat and the weeds both grow together until harvest'" (Matt 13:24–30 GN). The servants, and we, are told it is not our job to separate the bad from the good, to judge and single out the sinners. It is our task to love one another, to grow together, to learn to live together, and to trust that God knows what he is doing and will sort things out in his own good time.[1]

The second challenge to our ability to cope with Sin is that we are side-tracked by our misunderstanding of Christianity as a matter of correct belief and proper behavior (see chapter 1). The only additional point to be made here is that sins are a matter of breaking hearts rather than breaking rules.

Some years ago, I watched a movie that puts this matter into proper perspective. *Defending Your Life* is a 1991 comedy with a surprisingly good Christian message. It was written and directed by Albert Brooks, who also played the lead role. Meryl Streep played the female lead. In an early scene, Daniel, played by Brooks, purchases a new BMW convertible, has a head-on collision with a bus, and is killed. He awakens in Judgment City, and soon finds that he will have to defend his life. What is so accurate in terms

---

1. Capon, *Kingdom, Grace, Judgment*, 86.

of good Christian teaching is that Daniel is not to be judged on the basis of his Sin or his sins, not on the rightness of his behavior and not on the correctness of his beliefs. As the story unfolds, he is judged on whether he had lived as a fearful person. The concept, the theology, is that fear is the opposite of trust. A person with faith in God would trust God and not be fearful. While in Judgment City, Daniel meets Julia, played by Streep, and they fall in love. In the climax of the story, through his love for Julia and her love for him, Daniel overcomes his fears. He is judged on his trust in God and saved by love. This is excellent, even biblical, theology.

The remedy for Sin and for sins, difficult though it may be, is trust, trust in God. The restorative is trust in a relationship that, from God's side, is an accomplished fact, accomplished in the life of Jesus. Jesus revealed and represented God's love. In representing God, Jesus was more troubled by, and critical of, the leaders of his people, than he was by those labeled sinners. In Mark's Gospel Jesus was criticized for associating with those so-called sinners. "Some doctors of the law who were Pharisees noticed him eating in this bad company, and said to his disciples, 'He eats with tax-gatherers and sinners!'" (Mark 2:16 NEB). Jesus' reply to his critics carries the point being made here. "Jesus heard it and said to them, 'It is not the healthy that need a doctor, but the sick; I did not come to invite virtuous people, but sinner.'" (Mark 2:17 NEB). St. Paul drives this home: "But God has shown us how much he loves us—it is while we were still sinners that Christ died for us!" (Rom 5:8 GN). The acceptance, the invitation to trust, is there, always, before we make a move.

Why is it so difficult for us to accept God's acceptance? Our drive for self-preservation becomes a self-concerned assertiveness that causes separation, and loneliness, and isolation even from God. That self-centeredness is named Sin. Its consequences are the things we do, and fail to do, the sins that damage our relationships and make us miserable. When, though, two persons relate to one another lovingly and well, the spark of energy that occurs between them is of the nature of God. The space in which two persons relate openly and honestly is charged with the presence of God. God is in the relationship; God as love is the relationship.

SIDEBAR

Original Sin

THE DOCTRINE OF ORIGINAL sin lies behind the consideration of Sin and sins. This doctrine is problematic for the specific reason that it depends upon a literal interpretation of a mythical story in the third chapter of the book of Genesis. This misinterpretation, regarding myth as historical fact, plays out in numerous ways.

The mythical story begins, "Now the snake was the most cunning animal that the Lord God had made. The snake asked the woman, 'Did God really tell you not to eat fruit from any tree in the garden?' 'We may eat the fruit of any tree in the garden,' the woman answered, 'except the tree in the middle of it. God told us not to eat the fruit of that tree or even touch it; if we do, we die.' The snake replied, 'That's not true, you will not die'" (Gen 3:1–3 GN). Here are our first clues to this being mythology rather than historical fact. There is a talking animal, and even a conversation between this animal and a human. And there are two trees that bear magic fruit.

As the story unfolds, the woman and then the man eat the forbidden fruit of the tree in the middle of the garden. They did not die, "but were given understanding" (Gen 3:7 GN). They now know good and evil, and realize that they are naked and hide from God. With the knowledge of good and evil they lose their innocence, and their once innocent relationship with God becomes strained. They overreach themselves, reach for what is not theirs, and are evicted from the garden. This loss of the original and innocent relationship with God, which leads to their eviction, is called the fall of man. However, this fall was also a maturation into the knowledge and understanding that is the basis of human decisions and choices. Ironically, the fall may be considered a "fall upward." As a result of their overreaching, the man and woman gained the knowledge of good and evil and became fully human.

Their full human condition can be seen in a brief episode within the story. "God asked, 'Did you eat the fruit that I told you not to eat?' The man answered, 'The woman you put here with me gave me the fruit and I ate it'" (Gen 3:11b–13 GN). He blames the woman, and even blames God for having created the woman. And she blames the snake. "The Lord God asked the woman, 'Why did you do this?' She replied, 'The snake tricked me into eating it'" (Gen 3:13 GN). Everyone tried to shift the blame, as we do to this very day. Imagine the effect ducking and shifting blame has on our relationships.

In consequence of the disobedience of this mythical first man and first woman, a series of events unfold. The second magical tree is introduced: "Then the Lord God said, 'Now these human beings have become like one of us and have knowledge of what is good and what is bad. They must not be allowed to take fruit from the tree that gives life, eat it, and live forever'" (Gen 3:22 GN). They were expelled from the garden. "Then at the east side of the garden he put living creatures and a flaming sword which turned in all directions. This was to keep anyone from coming near the tree that gives life" (Gen 3:24 GN). This "tree that gives life" brings us back to the doctrine of original sin. One argument for this doctrine is that death is the result of Sin, and since all die, all must surely be sinful. This belief is found in the writings of St. Paul. "Sin came into the world through one man (Adam), and his sin brought death with it. As a result, death has spread to the whole human race because everyone has sinned" (Rom 5:22 GN). The argument is that death is ubiquitous because Sin is ubiquitous, and it all began with the fall. It would appear, though, that the man and woman in the garden, even before the fall, were destined to die. If they were destined to live forever there would have been no concern that they might "take fruit from the tree that gives life, eat it and live forever" (Gen 3:22b GN). The universality of death does not support the doctrine of original sin.

The doctrine of original sin also depends on accepting the man and woman in the creation story, Adam and Eve, as actual historical people who bequeath to all subsequent generations the consequences of the fall. According to this teaching, original sin is transmitted from one generation to the next because of concupiscence and through procreation. Original sin becomes a venereal disease, almost. How, though, can we inherit anything from mythical persons?

The doctrine of original sin is based on a literal reading of an ancient —Adam + Eve myth, claiming it to be history. That reading no longer makes sense. Scientific studies have shown that we are the result of a very long and slow development. The creatures we are today did not come into being complete and all of one piece. There were no first man and woman living in an idyllic garden, as described in the book of Genesis. And, as John Shelby Spong points out, without a time of "original perfection" there could not have been a fall from perfection into something called "original sin."[1] As myth, though, the story of that first man and woman relates profound truths about our human condition. We do live in a matrix of destructive self-centeredness, reaching for more than is ours. We do fear that we are naked and vulnerable. We do hide our true selves from one another. We do shift the blame to others when we can. We do break hearts. Relationships are difficult for us, but good relationships are always possible, and very few of our sins are very original.

1. Spong, *Unbelievable*, 83.

PART II

The Bible

4

Actors and Authors

I DON'T BELIEVE THE Bible was written by God. The Bible is our record of our relationship with God. Because it is a product of human endeavor, inconsistencies, contradictions, and errors can be found throughout the Bible. Little in this real world is flawless, which is particularly so once touched by human hands. A Bible that is less than perfect is more compatible with this less than perfect world, our world, where we live our lives and make our choices: some good, some bad, and some just irrelevant. To borrow and redirect a few words of President Lincoln, the Bible is of the people, by the people, and for the people. It is the story we have written of a relationship given, lost, and restored over and over again. The claim that it was written by God is an attempt to defend the Bible as without flaws, contradictions, or errors, despite the evidence that they exist.

The Bible is the classical record of the relationship between God and his creation. Its message needs to be made more accessible, and to do this I think all Holy Scripture must be approached as a product of human effort and ability, subject to human strengths and weaknesses, and human choices. This does not, in my estimation, in any way disparage the credibility or the importance of the Bible.

To begin, the Bible is a book, like any other book, printed on paper and bound, in some manner, within a cover. Then, also, the Bible is not a book. It is a number of books bound into one volume. It is a small library. This library in one volume, by one count, consists of sixty-six books (not including the Apocrypha), thirty-nine in the Old Testament and twenty-seven in the New Testament, written by forty authors over the course of 1,500 years. It is written in three languages: Hebrew, Greek, and Aramaic. The events recorded take place in 1,551 locations and involve 2,900 characters, or actors. These books include prose and poetry, mystery and romance, history and theology. When they were written, neither recorded history nor the study of science, as we know them today, had come into existence.

Because the Apocrypha is not well known, something should be said about it, and that will bring up the Septuagint. The Apocrypha (from Greek for "hidden") is the name given to fifteen books found in the Greek translation of the Hebrew Scriptures that are not in the original Hebrew Scriptures. The Septuagint (from Latin for "seventy") is the name given to the Greek translation of Hebrew Scriptures. It was given this numerical name because of a legend that it was translated by seventy scholars in seventy days. This translation actually took a long time, much of the third and second centuries BCE. The Septuagint is often designated by the Roman numeral for seventy, LXX. Most of this work of translation was done in Alexandria, Egypt.[1]

The books of the Septuagint and Apocrypha are important in the study of Christian Scriptures. When the Apocrypha is omitted from the Bible, we are deprived of a valuable source of information for those years that most closely preceded the life of Jesus. The books of the Apocrypha were written in that period of history between the writing of the Old Testament and the New. The last book of the Old Testament, the book of Daniel, was written around 165 BCE, and the first book of the New Testament, St. Paul's First Letter to the Thessalonians, was written around fifty CE. The Septuagint is also important because early Christian writers, including the authors of our New Testament books, relied upon and quoted the LXX rather than the Hebrew Scriptures. An illustration of this dependence on the LXX is found in Matthew's Gospel (1:23 GN). "A virgin will become pregnant and have a son, and he will be called Immanuel (which means, 'God is with us')." We see that Matthew is quoting from the LXX, because in Hebrew Scripture this verse reads, "Therefore the Lord himself shall give you a sign: A young woman is with child, and she will bear a son, and will call him Immanuel." (Isa 7:14 NEB). Only in the Greek translation is the young woman a virgin.

---

1. Cross and Livingston, eds., *Oxford Dictionary of the Christian Church*, s.v. "Septuagint."

For Judaism, First and Second Maccabees, the last two books in the Apocrypha, are important because they provide the historical background for Hanukkah, the celebration of the defeat of the Syrians and the rededication of the temple in Jerusalem in 164 BCE.

My introduction to a serious study of the Bible started two weeks before regular classes began for my first year of seminary. In those two weeks we were given a crash course in the Greek language in which the New Testament was written. Greek, at the time of Jesus, was the international language of commerce, government, and philosophy. As such, it acquired a sophisticated and difficult grammar. Then too, it is written in a different alphabet from English. Two weeks was too short a time, and too exhausting, to master a complex foreign language. When classes began, we were handed a Nestle-Aland Greek New Testament and told to read. That was a frightening experience.

We did all our New Testament studies in Greek. In those studies, I discovered that our heroes of the faith were real people with real fears, hopes, and foibles. They had their gifts and strengths, and also their weaknesses. They were not superhuman. That gave me some hope that I might be able to follow in their footsteps, if only in my own stumbling way. I saw that I, too, might have a ministry in Christ.

Discovering that the heroes of the faith, the actors as I am calling them, were genuine human beings led me to understand that the writers, the authors as I am calling them, were also genuine human beings. There is ample evidence that God was content with, or at least accepting of, many of the most notable biblical figures in their true and natural human condition. I offer these illustrations of the very human behavior of the actors.

According to the Old Testament, Abraham became the father of all Israel, and the source of blessing for all peoples, even though he was at times less than a commendable role model. We read in Genesis that at one stop on his journey to the promised land, out of fear for his life, Abraham lied by passing off his wife, Sarah, as his sister. "He said that Sarah his wife was his sister, and Abimelech king of Gerar sent and took her" (Gen 20:2 NEB). That put Sarah in a very difficult position and was not a very nice thing for Abraham to do. It was, though, a quite human thing to do.

To offer another example, Moses was a murderer; even so, God chose him to lead the Israelites out of Egypt. Moses "saw an Egyptian strike one of his fellow Hebrews. He looked this way and that, and seeing there was no one about, he struck the Egyptian down and hid his body in the sand"

(Exod 2:11b–12 NEB). Moses became God's spokesperson even though he tried to weasel out of what God was calling him to do by claiming a speech impediment. "But Moses said, 'O Lord I have never been a man of ready speech, never in my life, not even now that thou hast spoken to me; I am slow and hesitant of speech'" (Exod 4:10 NEB). None of this disqualified him.

The final example is David, who became the greatest of Israel's kings even though he was an adulterer who had the husband of his mistress, Bathsheba, killed in battle. David said, "Put Uriah opposite the enemy where the fighting is fiercest and then fall back and leave him to meet his death" (2 Sam 11:15 NEB). God chose Abraham, Moses, and David despite their very human shortcomings.

Turning to the New Testament, St. Peter alone is a sufficient example of God's acceptance of flawed actors. For one thing, St. Peter had a bad habit of opening his mouth before engaging his mind. After proclaiming Jesus to be the Messiah, he just could not leave well enough alone. When Jesus announced that he was going to Jerusalem to die, St. Peter took it upon himself to rebuke Jesus. Jesus put him in his place, even referring to him as a satan. This can be read in Mark's Gospel. Jesus "began to teach them that the Son of Man had to undergo great sufferings . . . be put to death. . . . At this Peter took him by the arm and began to rebuke him. . . . But Jesus turned round, and, looking at his disciples, rebuked Peter. 'Away with you, Satan,' he said" (Mark 8:31–33 NEB). At the arrest of Jesus, just prior to the crucifixion, St. Peter denied three times that he had had anything to do with Jesus. In the third denial, "bystanders said to Peter, 'Surely you are one of them. You must be; you are a Galilean.' At this he broke out into curses, and with an oath he said, 'I do not know this man you speak of'" (Mark 14:71 NEB). Even so, St. Peter became the leader of the twelve apostles and head of the Christian church in Rome. God accepted these men, the actors within the story, for who and what they were, and despite their very human proclivities they became great figures in the history of the Jewish and Christian faiths. God did not fire a single one of them.

It can be asked, why would God deal less graciously with those who recorded the stories than with those who were the actors in the stories? Would God have dealt with St. John as he wrote his Gospel any differently than he dealt with him as an apostle in the story? That is assuming John the apostle wrote the Gospel, which is questioned by some. Why would we suppose that God would require a perfection in the authors that he did not require in the actors? If St. Peter could be an actual human being in the story, quite open to making mistakes, why would St. Mark, in recording it, have to become some sort of superhuman unable to make a mistake, or choice, or be affected by the world around him? To actually write the Bible, God would have had to override the feelings, personality, and human qualities of the various authors. When considering the authors of the books of the Bible, considering God's acceptance of the actors, it is a mistake to think God would be coercive and manipulative with one while being loving and accepting of the other. I think God's loving-kindness is constant. It is inconsistent of us, and even derogatory, to claim that a loving God would violate our humanity for any reason. And it should be said that making a person superhuman is as much a violation as making that person subhuman.

The evidence of individual human authors is clear when accounts of the Last Supper are compared. In Mark's Gospel, Jesus' Last Supper with his disciples was a Passover meal, "Now on the first Day of Unleavened Bread, when the Passover lambs were being slaughtered, his disciples said to him, 'Where would you like for us to go and prepare for your Passover supper?'" (Mark 14:12 NEB). It is clear that Jesus and his disciples gather for a Passover meal because the story ends, "After singing the Passover Hymn, they went out to the Mount of Olives" (Mark 14:26 NEB). The Gospels of Matthew and Luke agree with Mark that the Last Supper was a Passover meal. John disagrees: "It was the eve of Passover, about noon." (John 19:14 NEB). Pilate tried to avoid having Jesus executed, but he was shouted down by the crowd: "Then at last, to satisfy them, he handed Jesus over to be crucified" (John 19:16 NEB). Noon would be the time the paschal lambs were slaughtered. In this Gospel, the crucifixion occurred on the day before the Passover, so the Last Supper could not have been a Passover meal. The author of John's Gospel introduced his concept of Jesus as the Lamb of God by having John the Baptist announce it at the beginning of his Gospel, "The next day he saw Jesus coming towards him. 'Look,' he said, 'there is the Lamb of God; it is he who takes away the sins of the world'" (John 1:29 NEB). Then he had Jesus crucified at the time that the Passover lambs were slaughtered. Evidently, the author of John's Gospel was free to do his own thing, to slightly alter the facts of the Last Supper to express what he believed to be the truth, that Jesus is the Lamb of God.

The authors of the four Gospels were gifted writers, inspired, but also influenced by their own concerns and by what was going on in the world around them. The early Christians were Jews whose world had collapsed. Their nation had been conquered by the Romans, and what was both the political and spiritual center of their lives, Jerusalem and the temple, had just been destroyed. In the year 70 CE their world had come to an end, and this is about the time the Gospel of Mark was written. Those first Christians, including the ones who wrote any part of the New Testament, were living in a turbulent time of stress and fear. Mark's Gospel is itself an example. Surely, one of the motivations for the writing of this Gospel was the destruction of Jerusalem and the temple.

The Bible, the book, is a very special book, but even so, a book written in much the same way as any other book. It is important to establish this approach to clarify how the Bible will be used throughout these pages. The claims that the Bible was written by God, that it is the literal words of God, that it is inerrant, are accepted by only a portion of Christianity. That approach to the Bible is detrimental to the acceptance of Christianity in this day and age. How it is detrimental will be explained in the following chapters.

My approach to the Bible has been to start with the people of the book, both actors and authors. Declaring that the Bible has many human authors rather than one divine authorship does not denigrate the Bible's validity. A Bible written by human authors is more in keeping with our experience with God, and more accessible to human readers. The relationship with God that the Bible portrays is our relationship written from our point of view and in our terms. The story the Bible tells is our story. And those who authored or edited any part of it had no idea they were writing Holy Scripture. Each was writing for the people of his own community, to inform, to guide, to uplift. What they wrote is serving its purpose to this day. They succeeded.

SIDEBAR

Biblical Background

THERE IS AN ADDITIONAL field of biblical study that precedes the translation of Holy Scriptures from the Hebrew and Greek in which they were originally written into any other language. This study deals with the problems arising from the fact that there are no original copies of any book in the Bible, Old Testament or New. We have only copies of copies of copies, among which there are many errors and even disagreements. There are thousands of manuscripts, and they date not from a few years after the events covered, but from many years later. The earliest surviving piece of a New Testament manuscript, and it is a very small piece, is a fragment of the Gospel of John 18:31–33 on one side and John 18:37–38 on the other. It is dated to around 125 to 150 CE, which puts it at least a quarter of a century or more after the Gospel was written. Most other manuscripts are from much later times.[1]

Prior to any translation into a modern language, a careful study of the manuscripts must be made, and a decision made as to which manuscripts are the most accurate. This process is even more difficult in those passages where it is not possible to determine what the original words and meaning may have been.

1. Ehrman, *New Testament.*

There are additional problems. Ancient Hebrew was written without vowels. Jewish grammarians known as the Massoretes[2] worked on the texts of the Old Testament from about the sixth century to the tenth century CE. Their work of providing vowels was probably completed about the year 900. The ancient Greek of the New Testament was written all in uppercase letters, without punctuation and with no spaces between paragraphs, sentences, or even words. The chapter divisions with which we are familiar are the work of Stephen Langton, who was the archbishop of Canterbury at the time of his death in 1228. The verse numbers with which we are familiar are the work of a Parisian printer, Robert Stephanus, in the middle of the sixteenth century.[3]

To illustrate some of the difficulties, how do you read the following phrase: "GODISNOWHERE"?

2. Cross and Livingston, eds., *Oxford Dictionary of the Christian Church*, s.v. "Massoretes."

3. Ehrman, *New Testament*, 24.

5

Inspiration and Possession

I DON'T BELIEVE GOD would violate our humanity. A loving God would not turn a human being into an android, into a puppetlike creature that would no longer be truly a human being. If God were to do that, it would be, in effect, a matter of possession rather than inspiration.

Possession is a dehumanizing control. It abrogates the freedom of choice that is at the core of being fully human. To be possessed is to be taken over, to lose much of what could be called personness. It is abusive. Inspiration is a gentle, supportive, loving guidance that does not strip a person of his or her humanity. Inspiration is the result of persuasion rather than coercion and control.

The issue at hand is God's relationship with us, and more specifically, with the various authors of Holy Scripture. If God is the author, outright, does that not relegate the human authors to the level of being some strange sort of human Dictaphones? Was their God-given freedom denied or otherwise voided, their freedom to choose removed by the very God who granted it? To transform any person into a superhuman creature, free from natural human foibles, is as dehumanizing as transforming a person into a subhuman creature. To err is human. We should take care not to imply that God would contravene our humanity. We should, instead, avow that a loving God would not tamper with our human nature, much less violate it, to accomplish his will. The outcome of an overzealous defense of a flawless

Bible becomes a denigration of God. Is an infallible book at the expense of a fallible God at all acceptable?

The evidence in the Bible shows a gentle inspiration, a divine guidance. Nothing more invasive is in evidence. The Christmas stories are offered here as illustrations because they are among the best-known stories in the Bible. They are certainly inspired, but also reveal the handiwork of two different authors, called Matthew and Luke. There is no indication of either being in any way manipulated by God.

When considering the Christmas stories, I recall my early experience of being charged with organizing the Christmas pageant at St Paul's Episcopal Church in New Orleans. At the time that I finished seminary, young clergy were assigned to a larger church where they could work under the supervision of a more experienced priest. In many instances the young seminary graduate was put in charge of youth ministry. In my case, the planning and organization of the Christmas pageant was a dreadful part of the youth program. Dreadful because parents who saw to it that their child never missed a practice session of whatever sport that child had been forced into, never saw a pageant rehearsal as of any importance at all. I came to believe that the lack of support was caused by a high level of familiarity but a superficial understanding of the nativity stories.

Christmas pageants are a blatant fusion of two distinct and different Christmas stories, one in Matthew's Gospel and the other in Luke's. Neither Mark's Gospel nor John's have a nativity story, and there is no mention of the birth of Jesus in the writings of St. Paul. Interlacing the two nativity stories in a Christmas pageant is now a matter of tradition. In its way, this mixture provides a good and broad picture of Jesus and the message of the Gospels. Matthew's Gospel, with the presentation of gifts by the star-guided magi, shows us the majestic significance of the birth and life of Jesus. Luke's Gospel, with the proclamation of the angels to the culturally marginalized shepherds, shows us the openness of Jesus to the least important and powerless, and to the inclusive nature of the gospel. The popularity of Christmas pageants, with their fusion of the two very different nativity stories, is evidence that we do not, and need not, take the Bible literally.

To clearly see the evidence of individual, personal decisions in the construction of the Christmas stories, with no evidence of anything like possession, we need to look at them in detail. I turn first to the Christmas story in Matthew's Gospel, 1:18–25 and 2:1–23. The main character is Joseph, guided by angels in his dreams. In the first such appearance, "an angel of the Lord appeared to him in a dream. 'Joseph son of David,' said the angel, 'do not be afraid to take Mary home with you as your wife. It is by the Holy Spirit that she has conceived this child'" (Matt 1:20 NEB). There is no actual account of the birth of Jesus, no census, no inn, no swaddling clothes, no stable, and no angels singing to frightened shepherds. Mary never says a word. The story moves from Joseph to Herod, who receives the magi in Jerusalem. The magi are never numbered; there being three gifts (gold, frankincense, and myrrh) led to an assumption that there were three magi. They find Jesus in a house, not a stable: "Entering the house they [the magi] saw the child with Mary his mother" (Matt 2:11 NEB). The story then returns to Joseph and his dreams, in which angels warn him to flee for the child's safety because Herod seeks to kill him. This is important: the journey of the Holy Family is from its home in Bethlehem, to Egypt, and then to Nazareth.

I turn now to the Christmas story in Luke's Gospel, 2:1–20. Mary the mother of Jesus is the main character in Luke's version of the story. An angel appears to Mary to announce the conception of Jesus by the power of the Holy Spirit. This was no dream. For Mary, a young unmarried girl, it must have seemed like a nightmare. In contrast to her silence in Matthew's narrative, Mary converses with the angel and then sings a song to the mother of John the Baptist. Joseph never says a word. It is in Luke's version of the Christmas story that we find the census, an inn with no vacancy, the manger, swaddling clothes, and a field full of shepherds astonished by the proclamation of the angels. There is no star and there are no magi. There is no mention of Egypt. This is important: because of a census, the journey of the Holy Family is from their home in Nazareth, to Bethlehem, and then back to Nazareth. The stories of the two journeys, one in Matthew and one in Luke, are clearly different.

When the two stories of the birth of Jesus, one in Matthew's Gospel and one in Luke's Gospel, are read with an eye on the details, it is obvious that they are two separate stories written by two different people, each with his own purpose for telling the story in his own way. There are elements in these stories that agree, but they are significantly different stories in details and in purpose.

The details have been reviewed above. Very briefly, the purpose of Matthew's Gospel was to present Jesus as the new Moses. As Moses led the Israelites out of Egypt, it is from Egypt that Jesus must arrive in Nazareth. And he is visited and given expensive gifts by persons of importance, the magi. Evidence of a presentation of Jesus as the new Moses is also seen in the five-part construction of the Gospel to model the Five Books of Moses, a name given the first five book of the Old Testament, once thought to have been written by Moses. Then, just as Moses went to the mountaintop to receive the law, Jesus presents his teachings, his law, from the mountaintop in the Sermon on the Mount. "When Jesus saw the crowds, he went up the mountain; and after he sat down, his disciples came to him" (Matt 5:1 NRSV). The purpose of Luke's Gospel was to portray Jesus as concerned foremost with the down-and-out who had been marginalized by the power structure of their society. His birth is announced to shepherds who lived on the outskirts of society. In this Gospel Jesus presents his teachings in a Sermon on the Plain, on level ground. "He came down with them and stood on a level place" (Luke 6:17a NRSV). In Luke's version, Jesus not only pledges his support for the poor, but offers fair warning to the well-to-do in a series of "woes" that are included in his version of the Beatitudes. Here is an example: "Then he looked up at his disciples and said, 'Blessed are you who are poor, for yours is the kingdom of God'" (Luke 6:20 NRSV). Then the tone changes: "But woe to you who are rich, for you have received your consolation" (Luke 6:24 NRSV).

These two accounts of the birth of Jesus do not need to agree in order to be true. To be true, they need not even to have happened. The importance of these stories does not depend upon their being historically factual. Their importance lies in the truth of their meaning. The meaning is that Jesus partook of the nature of God as no other person ever had. He brought God to us in a very personal way. For Matthew, Jesus is the new Moses to whom the mighty of heaven and earth bow down. For Luke, Jesus is most involved with the poor, the downtrodden, and the marginalized. Do not stumble over the facts and miss the meaning—the Bible always means what it means. Which is to say that some of this may not actually have happened, but that does not make it any less true and important. Both nativity stories are true in what they tell us about Jesus. This is inspired writing.

To further illustrate the word of truth in inspired writing, without reliance upon fact, I turn to two of the parables of Jesus. Consider the parable of the prodigal son (Luke 15:11–32). Briefly summarized, it is the story of a loving father who has two sons. The younger son recklessly wastes his inheritance and gets into such a jam that he has no choice but to return home. The father welcomes him with open arms, even before the son can make any excuses. The older son, who has been hard working, is upset by the reception his brother receives. The father now has two sons to assure of his acceptance and love. The truth and significance of the parable does not depend upon there having been a specific prodigal son with a name and address. That is not at all necessary. The meaning and power of this parable lies, rather, in the truth that each of us has at some time been a less than perfect son or daughter. It is just as reprehensible to behave like the prig of an older brother. I suggest that this parable speaks to realistic problems sometimes experienced in family relationships, and of God as a loving father.

I turn now to the parable of the good Samaritan (Luke 10:29–37). This parable is about a man who was waylaid by robbers, beaten and left half dead. Two persons, thought to be solid citizens, walk by without lifting a hand to help him. A Samaritan, despised and considered an enemy, came to his aid, and rescued him. This need not be a datable event with verifiable facts to be true. The meaning and power of this parable depends on the truth that we are all called upon to follow the example of the good Samaritan. What these two parables tell us about human nature, about ourselves, is no less true because they are stories, fiction rather than fact.

The Bible is true irrespective of its being historical or scientifically factual. The Bible is true irrespective of the human purpose and personal design we discover when reading it. A genuine human touch is evident from the book of Genesis at the beginning to the book of Revelation at the end. And the involvement of an immanent God is not denied because one accepts the unique, individual character of the human authors. There was no coercive manipulation, no possession, but there was certainly a kindly inspiration. The Bible is the record of our response to the activities of God among us. It is written by real people, gifted and inspired people, people living in a real world among real people. Those biblical authors reveal the influence of their world and of what was happening around them. We can even see their personalities and purposes as they respond to the experiences of God in their lives. The human touch enhances what was written, giving it more variety and depth, making it more accessible to everyday people in an everyday world. Real people, writing for the benefit of other real people, putting their relation to God into words, moves the Bible out of the realm of the mystical into the world we inhabit.

SIDEBAR

Facts and Truth

THE LITERAL-FACTUAL INTERPRETATION OF the Bible, which is thought by some to be an expression of "that old time religion," is a fairly modern approach. It is the result of the Enlightenment, that period commencing in the seventeenth century in which the scientific way of knowing and understanding was accepted over all others. The scientific explanation is now the commonsense view of creation. Now, for too many, if something cannot be weighed and measured, or given a location and date within history, it cannot be true. What is lost is any understanding that something can be true without having to be factual. When this scientific view of the world, that only what is supported by fact can be true, is applied to the Bible, there are one or the other of two responses. One, the Bible is rejected as untrue. Two, the Bible is defended by the claim that even what is unbelievable is somehow supported by scientific or historical fact. The first is a great loss and the second is absurd.

What I find ironic is that those who reject the Bible and those who defend it are approaching it from the same intellectual position. They are both children of the Enlightenment. They have both accepted a scientific worldview that requires truth to be supported by fact. One side rejects the Bible. It is of no consequence because its truths are not supported by fact. The other side defends the Bible. It is said to be factual, historically and scientifically, even when most unbelievable.

We need to live between these extremes, of either rejecting the Bible or defending it as something it is not. To do so we need to recognize that the Hebrew people, up to and including those who wrote the books of the New Testament, wrote their theology in stories rather than essays or learned dissertations. Stories use images and figures of speech drawn from the culture and worldview of the time and place of writing. The worldview of the centuries during which the Bible was written was very limited both historically and scientifically. Biblical images are often drawn from a belief that the world is flat and creation in layers. This view of creation is seen in the story of the ascension of Jesus. There are two accounts, written by the same person, Luke. In the Gospel (24:50–51 NEB), Luke wrote: "and in the act of blessing he departed from them." In Acts (1:9 NEB), Luke wrote: "When he said this, as they watched, he was lifted up, and a cloud removed him from their sight." The Gospel version, by being vague, has given precedence to the version found in Acts. Consequently, we have an image of Jesus going "up" toward a heaven thought to be physically above the earth and sky.

In many parts of the Bible, truths of our human condition, of our relationships with God and one another, are developed in stories that may not actually have happened but are beautiful and communicate profound truths. Let us not reject these stories when we find the images unbelievable or try to defend these images as something they are not. Images may be taken for what they are, without any need to accept them as somehow factual. Then, as well, we may supplement these stories with our own images. By doing so, we may provide a way for these stories to speak to our time, to a world that very much needs to hear them. A great gift of the Hebrew people was the ability to put their beliefs into story form, which is more open to various interpretations and applications than an expository composition.

I will bring this to a close with a story. The wise man of the village gathered the young men around the campfire so that he might instruct them in the history and lore of their tribe. He called for their attention, and when he had it, he said to them: "Listen to me. This is an important story that you need to learn and to remember. It is a true story, and some of it may actually have happened." We may say much the same of the Bible: It is true, and some of it did actually happen.

The Bible may be read in three ways, to 1) proclaim, 2) educate, and 3) edify. When a passage from the Bible is read aloud to a congregation at worship, the purpose is to proclaim the good news. When a passage is read to come to grips with its history, context, and meaning, the purpose is to educate. When a passage from the Bible is read to uplift and enlighten, the purpose is to edify. These three ways of reading the Bible are not exclusive of each other but overlap. For instance, a reading for proclamation may educate, or an educational study may edify. All these three ways are necessary, each having an important function in reading the Bible.

6

Even and Uneven

I DON'T BELIEVE IN the verbal inerrancy of the Bible. Biblical inerrancy, briefly stated, is a belief that within the Bible there are no disagreements, errors, or contradictions. Every word of the Bible is considered to be of divine origin and unquestionably correct. The problem with the belief in verbal inerrancy is that it will not hold up under a careful reading of Holy Scripture.

Concerning disagreements, we find one when considering the nature of the Last Supper. We read in Mark's Gospel: "So the disciples set out and went to the city and found everything as he told them; and they prepared the Passover meal. When it was evening, he came with the twelve" (Mark 14:16–17 NRSV). Matthew and Luke follow Mark's timeline in describing the Last Supper as a Passover meal. John's Gospel is different: "Now it was the day of Preparation for the Passover; and it was about noon." "Then he handed him over to them to be crucified" (John 19:14–16 NRSV). It was the day before Passover when Pilate handed Jesus over to be crucified, at the time when the Passover lambs were slaughtered. John's Gospel has no account of the Last Supper, and it is clear that Jesus was crucified on the day of preparation. That final meal could not have been a Passover meal.

Concerning errors, one is found in the nativity stories. In Matthew (2:1 NEB): "Jesus was born at Bethlehem in Judea during the reign of Herod." According to Luke's Gospel (2:2 NEB): "This was the first registration of its kind; it took place when Quirinius was governor of Syria." The registration required the holy family to travel from Nazareth to Bethlehem, where Jesus was born. The reign of Herod lasted from 37 to 4 BCE, whereas Quirinius did not become governor of Syria until 6 CE, ten years after the death of Herod. Either Matthew or Luke is in error. These, and other difficulties with a doctrine of verbal inerrancy, have been fully investigated by many students of Holy Scripture, and I find no need to examine this issue any further.

Concerning contradictions, there appears to be one concerning the length of Jesus' ministry. The Gospels of Matthew, Mark, and Luke imply that the ministry lasted only one year. John implies that the ministry lasted three years.

Turning to verbal inerrancy, one argument against the belief is the uneven level of inspiration found throughout the Bible. The claim that the Bible is divinely inspired is widely accepted. A test of anything being inspired is that it, in turn, inspires. It should have a positive influence, a good effect. It should illuminate and even transform, yet some passages of Holy Scripture inspire while others do not. A verbally inerrant Bible should exhibit a consistent level of inspiration. A single author, a divine author with the big picture, and without any hindrance from the ups and downs of life on this earth, should give us a constant and even level of inspiration. This is not the case. Again and again, we find a fluctuation in the level of inspiration that one might expect from a number of individual writers. The level of inspiration is clearly uneven.

In the Old Testament, we find the unevenness of inspiration that would be expected in books written by different individuals experiencing various levels of inspiration as they went about their task. First, a comparison between passages in the book of Genesis and in 2 Kings. Beginning with the book of Genesis: "Then the Lord God formed a man from the dust of the ground and breathed into his nostrils the breath of life. Thus, the man became a living creature" (Gen 2:7 NEB). This is a very moving passage. We have here an immanent God, a God who is getting his hands dirty in creating us, a God who has rolled up his sleeves and gotten, up to his elbows, into the "stuff" of creation. Then he shares his breath of life with us.

Both 1 and 2 Kings are interesting and important to anyone studying the histories of Israel and Judah. However, I do not see how the contents of either of these two books of the Old Testament could inspire a person to faith, hope, and charity. In sharp contrast to the passage from the book of Genesis is a section of 2 Kings that, in the RSV, is labeled "A Succession of Evil Kings." Much of this section is formulaic in structure. For brevity, only a few verses have been selected from 2 Kings. "In the seventeenth year of Pekah the son of Remaliah, Ahaz the son of Jotham, King of Judah, began his reign" (2 Kgs 16:1 RSV). "And he did not do what was right in the eyes of the Lord his God" (2 Kgs 16:2b RSV). A catalogue of the actions of Ahaz follows. There is then a concluding statement that is almost the same in the case of every king: "Now the rest of the acts of Ahaz which he did, are they not written in the Book of the Chronicles of the Kings of Judah?" (2 Kgs 16:19 RSV). This is the pattern for a series of accounts of kings in Israel and Judah. I find this uninspiring, even boring.

Moving on to another part of the Old Testament, in the Psalms, different levels of inspiration are again in evidence. There is a section in Psalms, the Cursing Psalms, from which few psalms are taken for use in Christian worship. These psalms, in no uncertain terms, call upon God to curse someone. "It was you, a man of my own sort, my comrade, my own dear friend, with whom I kept pleasant company in the House of God. May death strike them, and may they perish in confusion, may they go down alive into Sheol; for their homes are haunts of evil! But I will call upon God; the Lord will save me" (Ps 55:13–16 NEB). In contrast, I turn to Psalm 27, the first and last verses, "The Lord is my light and my salvation; whom should I fear? The Lord is the refuge of my life; of whom then should I go in dread?" (Ps 27:1 NEB), and "Wait for the Lord; be strong, take courage and wait for the Lord" (Ps 27:14 NEB). There is so obvious a difference in tone in these two psalms that no comment should be necessary. What makes the psalms interesting as examples is that they are the words of ordinary people. These words were formed in the mouths of humans and are ready-made for our mouths. They are very human expressions of a broad range of emotions. But reading about one person consigning another to death and eternity in Sheol is not particularly uplifting.

The unevenness of inspiration in the New Testament is equally clear. I compare the opening verses of Matthew's Gospel with John's Gospel. I begin with John: "In the beginning was the Word, and the Word was with God, and the Word was God. He was in the beginning with God; all things were made through him, and without him was not anything made that was made. In him was life, and the life was the light of men. The light shines in the darkness, and the darkness has not overcome it" (John 1:1–5 RSV).

This passage is rich and beautiful, suitable for meditation and study. Much more is found to think about when the translation just given, from the Revised Standard Version, is compared with that of the New English

Bible. Here is just a bit of the latter: "When all things began, the Word already was. The Word dwelt with God, and what God was, the Word was." This is subtle, but decidedly different.

Now turn to the genealogy in Matthew's Gospel: "Abraham was the Father of Isaac, and Isaac the father of Jacob, and Jacob the father of Judah and his brothers, and Judah the father of Perez and Zerah by Tamar, and Perez the father of Hezron, and Hezron the father Ram, and Ram the father of Aminadab, and Aminadab the father of Nahshon, and Nahshon the father of Salmon, and Salmon the father of Boaz by Rahab, and Boaz the father of Obed by Ruth, and Obed the father of Jesse, and Jesse the father of David the king" (Matt 1:2–6 RSV). At last, we are back on familiar ground with King David. The genealogy continues, however, following one unpronounceable name with another for ten more uninspiring verses. These verses are not unimportant, just boring, unless one is into a serious study of Matthew's portrayal of Jesus as a new Moses, and all that is implied by that concept. I will have more to say on that concept in the next chapter.

The epistles of St. Paul exhibit a high level of inspiration and a strong human and personal influence. The New Testament professor I studied under in seminary, Dr. John H. W. Rhys, called to our attention that many of St. Paul's epistles were dictated to a scribe or someone acting in that capacity. The clearest evidence that St. Paul used scribes is found in his Letter to the Romans: "I Tertius, who took this letter down, add my Christian greetings" (Rom 16:22 NEB). Dr. Rhys suggested that St. Paul would hear of a problem in one of the small Christian communities he had established and would cry out, "Take a letter!" He would begin to pace the floor and dictate, and in his concern his words would come tumbling out. The scribe, under the force of St. Paul's personality and upset, dared not look up to say, "Mr. Paul, Mr. Paul, I didn't quite get that." No, he would keep his head down and keep writing.

Try to translate St. Paul's Epistles from the Greek into English and you can believe what that New Testament professor said. In the Greek there are run-on sentences that go on and on. Some have no clear subject and others are just confusing. Though some passages in his letters are unclear, some of the most inspiring passages in the New Testament are found in the "genuine" writings of St. Paul (see the Sidebar following this chapter for comments on the genuine writings of St. Paul). Though the thirteenth chapter of St. Paul's First Letter to the Corinthians is shopworn from much use in weddings, it is a good example. I quote: "Love is patient; love is kind and envies no one. Love is never boastful, nor conceited, nor rude; never selfish, not quick to take offence. Love keeps no score of wrongs; does not gloat over other men's sins, but delights in the truth. There is nothing love cannot face; there is no limit to its faith, its hope, and its endurance. Love will never end" (1 Cor 13:4–7 NEB).

The human touch to be expected in the letters of St. Paul can be found all through the Bible. The uneven levels of inspiration, as illustrated in the comparisons above, indicate the influence of fallible human beings choosing what to write and how to go about the writing.

I move now from St. Paul to the last book in the New Testament. My first example of the inspiration of the Bible was taken from the book of Genesis, the first book in the Bible. Consider now the last book in the New Testament, the Revelation of John, the final book in the Bible. The Revelation of John may seem a peculiar book in which to look for an inspiring passage that is positive and uplifting. This book is filled with puzzling images, bizarre creatures, war, plagues, and seas of blood. It is the strangest book in the Bible and the most difficult to understand. Even before it was accepted into the New Testament it had been the subject of controversy. Most probably, the Revelation of John was written during the persecution of Christians during the reign of the Roman Emperor, Domitian (91 to 96 CE). The Revelation of John was not written to reveal the future, but to comfort Christians who were subject to persecution and suffering.

No matter its strangeness, this book offers hope to those who are suffering. A good example is: "I saw the holy city, new Jerusalem, coming down out of heaven from God, made ready like a bride adorned for her husband. I heard a loud voice proclaiming from the throne: 'Now at last God has his dwelling among men! He will dwell among them, and they shall be his people, and God himself will be with them. He will wipe every tear from their eyes; there shall be an end to death, and to mourning and crying and pain; for the old order has passed away!' Then he who sat on the throne said, 'Behold! I am making all things new!'" (Rev 21:2–5 NEB). And we may believe ourselves included, being made new. That so inspiring a passage can be found within all the turmoil and fearful imagery of the Revelation of John is another example of an unevenness of inspiration.

The examples above are used to show that the argument is not against divine influence, but only against any claim of verbal inerrancy. While recognizing the inspired and inspiring nature of the Bible, it is also reasonable to acknowledge that the level of inspiration from book to book, and even from passage to passage in the same book, can be very inconsistent.

This inconsistency, this unevenness of inspiration, may seem trivial. It is, though, evidence that the Bible was written by people. The uneven level of inspiration surely indicates that the various authors, though inspired and very good at gathering and organizing the information that was available, were quite normal people going about their tasks of selecting, choosing, and writing as would any other gifted writers. The Bible is a drama, an ongoing story of relationships bestowed, lost, and restored. It is a drama written by genuine persons, each struggling to find the right words to express his understanding of the relationship between himself, his community, and God. It is clear, even if not consistently so, that what they wrote is inspired and inspiring.

SIDEBAR

Fundamentalism
Paul and Mark

THE CONCEPT OF VERBAL inerrancy of the Bible is one of the five points of fundamentalist Christianity. The other four are: a biological virgin birth, a physical resurrection, a substitutionary theory of the atonement, and a bodily return of Christ in a second coming. Fundamentalism developed at the turn of the nineteenth to the twentieth century, in reaction to the evolutionary theories of Charles Darwin and new approaches to biblical study. The term itself comes from a series of tracts entitled "The Fundamentals," the first of which was printed in 1909.[1]

When considering St. Paul, it is helpful to recognize that he gets a bad rap from letters that he probably did not write. Three of the letters ascribed to St. Paul, 1 and 2 Timothy and Titus, were most likely written around the year 100, and not by St. Paul. St. Paul was a contemporary of Jesus, though somewhat younger. Also, if tradition is true, he was martyred in Rome long before the year 100, possibly before the year 65. Authorship of three other letters is disputed: Ephesians, Colossians, and 2 Thessalonians. That leaves seven genuine, or undisputed, letters: Romans, 1 and 2 Corinthians, 1 Thessalonians, Galatians, Philippians, and Philemon. Accepting this division of authorship will lead to a better understanding of St. Paul. Then, too, if God wrote the Bible, why blame St. Paul for anything that upsets you?

---

1. Cross and Livingston, eds., *Oxford Dictionary of the Christian Church*, s.v. "Fundamentalism."

When considering the Gospels, there is a wee bit of very interesting history. Though we are not sure who Mark was, there is testimony to his authorship of the second Gospel found in the writings of Papias, the bishop of Hierapolis in the early second century. Papias' lost work, *The Interpretation of the Oracles of the Lord*, which was probably written near the beginning of the second century, is made known to us from a quote by a fourth-century Christian historian, Eusebius. Papias, it seems, cited an elder named John concerning the origin of the Gospels.

Concerning the authorship of the Gospel according to Mark, Eusebius, citing Papias, wrote:

> This also the Presbyter said: Mark, having become the interpreter of Peter, wrote down accurately, though not in order, whatsoever he remembered of the things said or done by Christ. For he neither heard the Lord nor followed him, but afterward, as I said, he followed Peter, who adapted his teaching to the needs of his hearers, but with no intention of giving a connected account of the Lords discourses, so that Mark committed no error while he thus wrote some things as he remembered them. For he was careful of one thing, not to omit any of the things which he had heard, and not to state any of them falsely. These things are related by Papias concerning Mark.[2]

With Mark's possible lack of order in mind it is interesting to look at the opening verses of Luke's Gospel, "And so, Your Excellency, because I have carefully studied all these matters from their beginning, I thought it would be good to write an orderly account for you" (Luke 1:3 GN).

---

2. Eusebius, *Ecclesiastical History*, 65.

PART III

Jesus

7

Man and God

I DON'T BELIEVE THE incarnation introduced something new. We believe in an immanent God, with us always and everywhere, and so the incarnation is not an instance of God showing up where he had not been before. It was a clear, most clear and most personal, revelation of God's constant presence. It is the visible instance of God's timeless pursuit of reconciliation.

The incarnation, briefly, is the doctrine of the church that in the man Jesus, God took on human flesh. Jesus was God with flesh, "God con carne," God incarnate. According to this doctrine, Jesus was fully human and fully divine. The word "completely" could be substituted for "fully." As completely human and divine, Jesus was 100 percent of each. It was not a fifty/fifty division. This is problematic when taken too literally or mechanistically. The belief behind this doctrine emerged very early, in the formative years of Christianity. Historically, agreement as to how to express this doctrine was not settled until the Council of Nicaea (325 CE) and the Council of Chalcedon (451 CE). The definition that came out of those two councils declared Jesus to be one person in two natures, united inseparably but without any intermingling. This definition is still open to discussion.

In that discussion, it helps to recognize that the incarnation is a verbal image. When we say Jesus is God, say that he is divine, we are using metaphors. A metaphor is a figure of speech in which a term is used for something to which it is not applicable in a literal sense. Metaphors say more, not less, than a restrictive literalism. Metaphors provide flexibility and depth of meaning as we try to use words to define concepts beyond our full understanding and the reach of our language.

Due to the difficulty of conceiving a person to be both human and divine, Christians have tacked back and forth, at one time defending the humanity of Jesus to the detriment of his divinity, at another time defending his divinity to the detriment of his humanity. In my experience, his divinity is now stressed to the detriment of his humanity.

During my last semester of college, I joined the National Guard. Upon graduation, I was attached to the Army for six months active duty for training, which began at Fort Chaffee, Arkansas. Following basic training, I was sent to Fort Sam Houston, San Antonio, Texas, to be trained as a medic and ambulance driver. Much of the time I spent at Fort Sam Houston could be described by the adage "Hurry up and wait." To fill the times of waiting, I read, which led me to carry a book with me most of the time, sequestered within my shirt. What I chose to read were those books of fiction about Jesus and his disciples: *The Day Christ Died* by Jim Bishop; *The Big Fisherman* by Lloyd Douglas; *Quo Vadis* by Henryk Sienkiewicz; and the like. Soon, I realized that the Jesus in these books was a magical figure. He knew everything that was going to happen to him and knew it in great detail. He was more wonder worker than actual person. Eventually, I saw some of the movies based on these books. In them, Jesus walked the dusty roads of the Holy Land in a white robe that remained clean and white throughout the movie. His sandaled feet never became dirty, much less sore. Jesus was not completely human.

Sometime later, after finishing my six months of active duty, after teaching school and working as a carpenter's helper, I entered seminary at the school of theology of the University of the South in Sewanee, Tennessee. Following seminary, at some time in the mid-1960s, I read *The Last Temptation of Christ*, by Nikos Kazantzakis. In his book Jesus is portrayed as fully human. Because of that portrayal, this book and the movie based on it raised the ire of many good churchgoing folk. I loaned my copy to a friend, and his wife came upon it and began to read it. She was so disturbed by it that she went to her priest with it. Upon learning that it was not on any forbidden list, she proceeded to burn my book. The Jesus in it was just too human for her, and she was not alone in her opinion. Her husband, I must add, was good enough to buy me another copy.

More people might benefit from reading that book. Because, whatever else is claimed for Jesus, his humanity, as being natural and complete and no different from ours, must be defended. Jesus was a real person, different from us in degree rather than in kind. Like the rest of us, he had only one brain. He had only a human brain to understand his divinity. He did not have two brains, nor did he have one brain with two compartments, one human and one divine, with the capability of "texting" questions and answers back and forth. He was a "standard-issue"[1] human. It is only natural that Jesus would have gone through stages of development just as would any person. He would have matured and grown, over time, into an understanding of who he was and what his life was to be. Perhaps that is why his public ministry did not begin until he was about thirty years old. "Jesus was about thirty years old when he began his work" (Luke 3:23 NRSV).

The Gospels, in various ways, allude to Jesus' human nature. Matthew's Gospel (1:1–17) and Luke's Gospel (3:23–38) include genealogies that position Jesus within a historical succession of persons. Matthew records an accusation that Jesus was "a glutton and a drunkard, a friend of tax collectors and sinners!" (Matt 11:19b NEB). That accusation is repeated in Luke's Gospel, word for word (Luke 7:34b NEB). These are accusations directed at Jesus because of his practice of eating with sinners. He was being too compassionately human in his association with those considered the dregs of society, those marginalized by the power structure of the day.

In Mark's Gospel there are two events recorded that imply that the contemporaries of Jesus (including members of his immediate family) viewed him as a person much like themselves. Jesus was in his hometown, teaching in the synagogue, and not being received well at all. "'Is not this the carpenter, the son of Mary, and brother of James and Joseph and Judas and Simon, and are not his sisters here with us?' And they took offense at him" (Mark 6:3 NRSV). More dramatic is the occasion when he was at home and attacked as being possessed. A large crowd had gathered. "When his family heard it, they went out to restrain him, for the people were saying, 'He has gone out of his mind'" (Mark 3:21 NRSV). In neither of these instances was Jesus considered to be divine.

There is further evidence in the Gospels of the completely human nature of Jesus. One is his admission that he did not know all things. He was not omniscient. When speaking of the end of heaven and earth, Jesus said, "But about that day or hour no one knows, neither the angels in heaven, nor the Son, but only the Father" (Mark 13:32 NEB). The ignorance of Jesus in

---

1. Felton and Procter-Murphy, *Living the Questions*, 183.

this and other instances underscores his participation in the normal limitations of human existence.

When considering the limits of Jesus' knowledge, one must look at those passages in the Gospels in which Jesus makes specific statements concerning his future. Here is a prime example: "They were on the road, going up to Jerusalem, Jesus leading the way; and the disciples were filled with awe, while those behind were afraid. He took the Twelve aside and began to tell them what was to happen to him. 'We are now going to Jerusalem,' he said; 'and the Son of Man will be given up to the chief priests and the doctors of the law; they will condemn him to death and hand him over to the foreign power. He will be mocked and spat upon, flogged and killed; and three days afterwards, he will rise again'" (Mark 10:32–34 NEB). No person could know his, or her, future in such detail. Why did the authors of the Gospels put words into the mouth of Jesus that are detrimental to his being considered a "standard-issue" human being? This was a way of proclaiming the very special nature of this man, and that they had come to believe and to accept his very special relationship to God. Recall that they were writing after the fact when the details of Jesus' life were known. As we read passages such as this, in which Jesus knows more than is humanly possible, it is important to see that portraying Jesus as superhuman is just as detrimental to his true humanity as it is to portray him as subhuman. Our destiny as human beings can be found in Jesus only to the extent that he was truly, completely human, a person like us in his humanity. This is expressed well in the Epistle to the Hebrews, "And therefore he had to be made like these brothers of his in every way, so that he might be merciful and faithful as their high priest before God, to expiate the sins of the people" (Heb 2:17 NEB).

To the degree that any powers are ascribe to his humanity that lift it to a level above and beyond that of other persons, to just that degree we can no longer find in him any relation to ourselves. Jesus' passion in the garden of Gethsemane is an example. It is either evidence of his true humanity, with no clear knowledge of his future, or it is only play acting. "And he took Peter and James and John with him, and he said to them, 'My heart is ready to break with grief; stop here, and stay awake'" (Mark 14:33–34 NEB). His life, death, and resurrection would not hold out any hope for us if he were not human in every way that we are. Whatever is said of Jesus, his humanity must be kept intact.

When considering the divinity of Jesus, it is equally important that it also be kept intact. Here, though, we have a problem. We don't fully know what we mean when we say "God is God." How can we fully understand what we mean when we say, "Jesus is God"? How can a human being be God? When we say, "Jesus is divine," we are saying something we can never fully understand and never adequately put into words. An examination of the divinity of Jesus would best begin by acknowledging that the incarnation is not a "fixed piece," something ready made by God and lowered into history from above. Rather than consider the incarnation as something, or someone, inserted into history as a rescue mission, it should be considered a manifestation of the dynamic character of God's enduring presence always and everywhere.

When the incarnation is approached from above, with the transcendence of God foremost in mind, it is difficult to see it as other than an isolated intervention. The result is then a mechanical explanation about how God set aside, divested himself of some of his divine attributes: omniscience, omnipotence, being everywhere present. When, however, the incarnation is approached from below, with the immanence of God foremost in mind, it becomes evident that Jesus set aside, overcame, the human attributes of self-centered selfishness, the I, me, mine disposition so natural to human nature. This, too, is a simple and mechanical explanation, but called for because the human side of the person of Jesus is so seldom considered.

It was not despite his humanity that Jesus revealed the presence of God. It was in his humanity, by his being a self-effacing and compassionate person. Jesus was criticized for eating with all sorts of people. "Some doctors of the law who were Pharisees noticed him eating in this bad company, and said to his disciples, 'He eats with tax collectors and sinners!'" (Mark 2:15–16 NEB). He turned no one away. It was from their experience with Jesus as a very special person that the disciples began to see the divine in the human. The man, Jesus, became the vehicle in which the presence of the divine could be engaged.

To ask when the human and divine came together in the incarnation, when it took place in the life of Jesus, is a misleading question, an unanswerable question. In Mark's Gospel it is written that the Spirit of God entered Jesus at his baptism. "It happened at this time that Jesus came from Nazareth in Galilee and was baptized in the Jordan by John. At the moment when he came up out of the water, he saw the heavens torn open and the Spirit, like a dove, descending upon him" (Mark 1:9–10 NEB). The Gospels of Matthew and Luke, by their nativity stories, imply that the incarnation took place at the birth of Jesus. John's Gospel, by means of its prologue, implies that Jesus is the incarnation of the eternal Word of God. "When all things began, the Word already was. The Word dwelt with God, and what God was, the Word was. The Word, then, was with God at the beginning, and through him all things came to be; no single thing was created without him. All that came to be was alive with his life, and that life was the light of men. The light shines on in the dark, and darkness has never mastered it" (John 1:1–5 NEB). I prefer the metaphorical opening of John's Gospel because it is less subject to literal, mechanistic explanations. This prologue (John 1:1–18) is a poem of timeless praise to God.

Not only are there different versions of when Jesus became divine, there are different versions of how this came about. For Mark it was by baptism, when Jesus saw the spirit "coming down on him like a dove" (Mark 1:10 GN). For Matthew and Luke, it was at his birth, as Mary was to "have a baby by the Holy Spirit" (Matt 1:18 GN). For John, "The Word became a human being and, full of grace and truth, lived among us" (John 1:14 GN).

To begin with a completely human Jesus is to move from the mechanical to the personal. It was through a natural human process of maturation that the human and divine in Jesus came together. The human and the divine in Jesus can be understood in terms of a dynamic, growing relationship rather than a static category. The incarnation is always in process. Also, the realization of the divinity of Jesus is not found at the beginning of the story, but at its climax, the resurrection. It was the disciples' experiences with Jesus that eventually led to their full awareness of who and what he was. It was a discovery that grew out of their relationship with him.

James, the brother of Jesus, is a good illustration of a growing realization culminating at the end of a process. This can be seen by connecting a few dots in Mark's Gospel and then turning to St. Paul. In Mark, Jesus goes home to Nazareth, and the crowd that gathers is so large that Jesus' family becomes alarmed and wants to restrain him (Mark 3:19b–21). Just a few verses later Jesus' mother and brothers, "standing outside" (Mark 3:31 NRSV), attempted to call him home, away from his public ministry. James is then listed as one of the brothers of Jesus (Mark 6:3 NRSV). It is no great leap to assume that James was among those family members who were troubled by Jesus' activities. A more direct expression of his family's doubts is found in John's Gospel: "For not even his brothers believed in him" (John 7:5 NRSV). Now turn to St. Paul's Letter to the Galatians, in which James is identified as an apostle. St Paul wrote, "but I did not see any other apostle except James the Lord's brother" (Gal 1:19 NRSV). There has been a significant shift in the attitude of James, from concern and doubt to belief, that developed over time. This shift in the attitude of James is an illustration of the gradual change in attitude that took place among the disciples.

It was a process that came to a climax in the words of St. Thomas, "My Lord and my God!" (John 20:28 NEB). Whether or not this statement is historically factual, it is theologically true when understood metaphorically. No one can know clearly what is meant when a person is declared a God.

N. T. Wright wrote: "I do not think that Jesus knew he was Divine."[2] He could not know, in any simple and direct way. Continuing to rely on the words of Wright, what Jesus experienced was a call, a vocation, to "do and be" what only God could "do and be." The disciples were witnesses to what Jesus was doing, and that led them to see God in the humanity of Jesus.

It is said that the secret name of God is Compassion. And, as recorded in the Gospels, Jesus was accepting and open to all sorts of people, inviting and compassionate. The presence of God was manifest in the compassionate humanity of Jesus. Consequently, the disciples eventually found themselves thinking of Jesus in terms they had traditionally reserved for God, giving birth to the concept of incarnation.

However, for the incarnation to be of consequence today it must become more than a piece of ancient history that took place in a foreign land. It must become, in us as in the disciples, a growing awareness of the consequences of the life of Jesus. Those consequences operate through participation. What is meant by participation is found in John's Gospel: "as thou, Father, art in me, and I in thee, so also may they be in us, that the world may believe that thou didst send me" (John 17:21b NEB). As Jesus participated in the nature of God, we participate in the nature of Jesus. Here we have a dynamic conceptualization of the incarnation.

---

2. Wright, *Simply Christian*, 119.

SIDEBAR

Evaluating the Creeds

THE CREEDS OF THE church are classic expressions of Christian doctrine. This should not, however, put them "out of bounds" for periodic evaluation, but make systematic study of them even more important. They are, after all, human creations, explanations, and definitions devised in the history of Christianity to meet particular challenges and problems. In different periods of history, the church faces different challenges, which then call for the doctrines of the church to be revisited and reevaluated. The creed produced at the Council of Nicaea was amended just over a century later by the Council of Chalcedon.

Because of its prominence, the Nicene Creed provides the better example for examination. In consequence of its being recited during services of worship in many churches, the Nicene Creed has the most influence on how the Christian faith is understood. This creed takes its name from the Council of Nicaea, which produced it in the year 325. The challenge at that time was Arianism. Arius, who lived from about 250 to 336 CE, and his followers denied the divinity of Jesus. Consequently, the Nicene Creed concentrates on defending the divinity of Jesus. It certainly accomplishes that purpose, but at the expense of saying very little about his humanity. The Nicene Creed does affirm that Jesus "became incarnate from the Virgin Mary and was made man. For our sake he was crucified under Pontius Pilate; he suffered death and was buried." Pontius Pilate was the Roman governor who ruled over Judea from about 26 to 36 CE. The creed moves immediately from the birth of Jesus to his death. Nothing is said of Jesus' ministry, his teachings and healings, his relationship with his disciples, or his attitude toward other people. It is out of balance. Some form of supplement is needed to support the humanity of Jesus to the degree that his divinity is supported. At our time in history, the acceptance of the humanity of Jesus needs more full attention and affirmation.

The divinity of Jesus is strongly affirmed, but this, too, needs consideration. For example, the Nicene Creed declares Jesus to be "God from God, Light from Light, true God from true God." These phrases are verbal images of the relationship of Jesus to God. To say that Jesus is "Light from Light" is clearly a metaphor. Jesus was not "light" in any visual sense, as would be a candle, light bulb, or any other source of light to human eyes. There is a depth of meaning in these phrases that is found when they are accepted as images of the presence of God experienced in Jesus. The Nicene Creed is as much poetry as it is prose, an essay in imagery. The more literally it is read the more is lost.

Here, at the end of these few comments on the Nicene Creed, I return to its beginning, to its first two words: "We believe . . ." In current usage, the word "believe" has come to mean a mental exercise, an intellectual process. The effect of this understanding of "believe" is that it turns the creed from being an affirmation of God into an explanation of God. It would be far better if we were affirming our relationship with God in Christ, rather than ideas about God and Christ. This could be accomplished by changing "We believe" to "We trust." With this one small change the creed becomes more than intellectual assent. It becomes an affirmation of faith. When we read or recite the Nicene Creed in worship we are saying, "I bet my life on this being so." We don't just believe that these ideas about God are correct, "We trust one God, the Father, the Almighty."

8

Resurrection or Resuscitation

I DON'T BELIEVE JESUS came back from the dead. It is clear in the Gospels that he did not resume the life he had before his death on the cross. The Gospels report that he did things impossible for a corporeal body, such as mysteriously appearing and disappearing. They repeatedly say that he was different enough that the disciples did not recognize him. Evidently, he was not simply resuscitated. Jesus moved ahead, beyond the confines of normal human life, into a new relationship with God. "The Lord is risen" is a metaphor for what occurred. Resurrection is a metaphor by which we reach beyond this life into a way of living we hope for but know nothing about. Jesus did not come back, he went on. He was the "pioneer and perfecter of our faith" (Heb 12:2 NRSV).

Resuscitation is not the same thing as resurrection. It is a coming back. Resuscitation is a return to life, a restoration of life, but with the realization that at some future date death will inevitably occur. Death has not been overcome, only postponed. Resurrection does not bring a person back only to face death again, but moves a person on into a new and more full relationship with God.

Immortality of the soul is also a concept quite different from resurrection. It is a concept taken from Greek philosophy in which the death of the body sets the soul free. The body was considered a physical impediment to be discarded. Resurrection is grounded in the biblical concept that both body and soul are created by God, and that both are essentially good. Life after resurrection is not a disembodied existence. St. Paul put it this way: "we shall not find ourselves naked" (2 Cor 5:3b NEB). The immortality of the soul is considered an inherent aspect of human nature whereas resurrection is a gift from a loving God. Two issues arise when considering the resurrection: the nature of the resurrection appearances and the nature of the resurrected body. These issues go to the heart of any consideration of resurrection. Considering first the nature of the resurrected body, the accounts in the New Testament are mixed and confused. There are the resurrection stories that present the risen Christ as having a fully physical body. In Matthew's Gospel, the women who went to the grave encountered a flesh and blood Jesus. "Suddenly Jesus was there in their path. He gave them his greeting, and they came up and clasped his feet, falling prostrate before him" (Matt 28:9 NEB). Evidently, the body of Jesus was corporeal and touchable. How, then, do we account for the disciples not being convinced by what they saw when they encountered Jesus in Galilee, for "some were doubtful" (Matt 28:17b NEB)? There is always a difficulty, a "but."

In John's Gospel we find a story that contradicts what is read in the passage from Matthew. John's account begins with Mary of Magdala, who saw Jesus "but did not recognize him" (John 20:14b NEB). She thought he was the gardener. "Jesus said to her, 'Do not cling to me, for I have not yet ascended to the father'" (John 20:17a NEB). In one Gospel, Matthew's, Jesus is touchable, in another, John's, he is not, or not so in this incident.

The Gospel according to John contains some of the more corporeal resurrection appearances, but none of them escape a mystical overlay. The more well-known story of doubting Thomas is found in this Gospel. According to the story, Thomas was invited to touch the risen Christ. Thomas had been absent from a previous appearance, and when told of it, doubted that it actually occurred. "A week later his disciples were again in the room, and Thomas was with them. Although the doors were locked, Jesus came and stood among them saying, 'Peace be with you!' Then he said to Thomas, 'Reach your hand here and put it in my side'" (John 20:24–29 NEB). Even though Thomas was invited to touch what is presented to him as a physical body, it is not a normal human body. As he approached Thomas, Jesus was not obstructed by walls and locked doors.

There is a third resurrection story in John's Gospel. In this story, Jesus serves as a chef for the disciples, preparing bread and fish, and evidently building a fire. It, too, begins in doubt because Jesus is not recognized: "Morning came, and there stood Jesus on the beach, but the disciples did not know that it was Jesus" (John 21:4 NEB). It was some time before he was recognized, which is a recurring theme in the Gospels.

In Luke's Gospel, there is the story of two men on their way to Emmaus, a village a few miles from Jerusalem. Jesus joined them and walked with them, but they didn't recognize him until they came to the end of their journey. When they reached their destination, the men invited Jesus to stay with them. "And when he sat down with them at table, he took bread and said the blessing; he broke the bread and offered it to them. Then their eyes were opened, and they recognized him; and he vanished from their sight" (Luke 24:30–31 NEB). This story is more about the liturgy of the Eucharist than about the resurrection, and most probably comes from a somewhat later time than the other resurrection stories. One indication of the liturgical nature of this story is that the recognition of Jesus followed the invitation "stay with us" (Luke 24:30 NEB). An even more clear indication of the liturgical nature of this appearance is that Jesus is recognized in the act of blessing the bread and wine. And, again, there is evidence that the body of Jesus was different, and not a normal human body medically resuscitated. In many of the resurrection stories Jesus appears and disappears rather mysteriously. In this story, "he vanished from their sight" (Luke 24:31 NEB).

The resurrection story found in Luke's Gospel that follows the encounter on the road to Emmaus is another about the women who went to the grave and encountered the risen Christ. They think they are seeing a ghost. Jesus says to them, "It is I myself. Touch me and see; no ghost has flesh and bones as you can see that I have" (Luke 24:39 NEB). Could they, did they touch him? Two verses later, "they were still unconvinced."

In these resurrection stories the body of Jesus is presented as a material body, but one that has nonmaterial qualities. In each resurrection story, the physical nature of the body of Jesus is compromised by the difficulty his followers have in recognizing him and by the mystical way in which he appears and disappears, vanishes. The authors of the Gospels are trying to describe experiences for which they have no words, and in trying to establish the reality of the risen Christ they tell stories in which the meaning is beyond the telling. The resurrection experiences are not as straightforward as the church's teachings often represent them. In Matthew's Gospel the disciples made their way to Galilee, to where Jesus had told them to meet him, and, "When they saw him, they fell prostrate before him, though some were doubtful" (Matt 28:17 NEB). In Luke's Gospel, Jesus appeared among the disciples as they were talking together, but, "They were still unconvinced, still wondering, for it seemed too good to be true" (Luke 24:41 NEB). In John's Gospel the disciples were so discouraged they went back to their old way of life: "Simon Peter said, 'I am going fishing.' 'We will go with you,' said the others" (John 21:3a NEB). There is confusion and doubt within the stories that lead to confusion, doubt, and even skepticism in our time. The more corporeal appearance stories, those that present the risen Christ as having a body of flesh and bone, are detrimental to the acceptance of the resurrection in this day and age. Rather than foster belief in the Christian message, they hinder it.

Therefore, I turn to St. Paul and the Corinthians. Corinth was a Greco-Roman city reestablished by Julius Caesar in 44 BCE. St. Paul's letter to the Christian community there is thought to have been written sometime around the year 55 CE, which would date it ten to fifteen years before Mark's Gospel, the earliest Gospel to be written. In the First Letter of Paul to the Corinthians we have the earliest account of the resurrection. In this letter, St. Paul is very pointed in his comments on the nature of the resurrected body. He writes, "But, you may ask, how are the dead raised? In what kind of body? How foolish!" (1 Cor 15:35–36 NEB). St. Paul continues with various illustrations, using different kinds of flesh, heavenly bodies, and seeds. "So it is with the resurrection of the dead. What is sown in the earth as a perishable thing is raised imperishable. Sown in humiliation, it is raised in glory; sown in weakness, it is raised in power; sown as an animal body, it is raised a spiritual body" (1 Cor 15:42–44 NEB). St. Paul goes as far as to say, "Flesh and blood can never possess the kingdom of God" (1 Cor 15:50 NEB). It is clear that St. Paul, by claiming that a body of flesh and blood cannot enter the kingdom of God, and that the body raised in resurrection is a spiritual body, argues against any notion of the resurrection of Jesus being a medical miracle that brought back from the dead a body of flesh and blood. From these writings of St. Paul, it is a short and easy step into accepting a bodily resurrection without requiring that it be a flesh and blood body. Here we need a new definition of body, as perhaps something we can use and by which we can be recognized.

In our time, even when the presence of Jesus is accepted, hope for a vision of, or an encounter with, a real corporeal Jesus is out of the question. If only such full-body-contact encounters qualify, we have little hope of experiencing resurrection. For us to trust in the continual presence of a risen Christ among us, he must be detached from images of a flesh and blood body.

I have found a commentary on the resurrection in a relatively new and unusual practice, when a deceased person is cremated. It is not with the acceptance of cremation itself that I find anything remarkable. It is in the disposition of the ashes that there is something new. I retired in 1998, twenty-plus years ago at this writing. During those years I have served several parishes along the Mississippi Gulf Coast as interim rector. The curious thing I have witnessed is that families of the deceased will sometimes bring several small containers to use in parceling out the ashes among family members. The ashes are taken all over the country and even off to foreign lands. This is not a rejection of the church's teachings on resurrection; it is a basic confusion regarding the general concept of resurrection. A growing number of persons simply find no place in their thoughts, one way or another, for any consideration of resurrection. It is simply ignored. Any insistence on believing the risen Christ had a corporeal body only makes matters worse. To the degree that resurrection of the body is a linchpin in Christianity, there is evidence here of a serious problem.

Turning to the other issue, the nature of the appearances, St. Paul provides the only primary source we have. He experienced a resurrection appearance. All Gospel accounts of the resurrection appearances are secondary sources. In Mark's Gospel there is no mention of any resurrection appearance. The authors of the other three Gospels are writing about the experiences of other persons. No one of them, so far as we know, was a witness to any appearance of the risen Christ. The authors of the four Gospels were all second-generation Christians.

In 1 Corinthians, St. Paul is to the point when writing about the resurrection appearances. Jesus, he wrote, "appeared to Cephas, and afterwards to the Twelve. Then he appeared to over five hundred of our brothers at once, most of whom are still alive, though some have died. Then he appeared to James, and afterwards to all the apostles. In the end he appeared even to me" (1 Cor 15:5–8 NEB). What is of interest here is that St. Paul considers the resurrection experiences of the disciples and his own experience on the road to Damascus as being of the same type. (For St. Paul's conversion experience on the road to Damascus, see the Acts of the Apostles 9:1–9; 22:6–11; 26:12–19.) St. Paul ties his experience to the experiences of the disciples by using the same word to describe them all, "appeared." Jesus appeared to them just as Jesus had appeared to him. In the Greek of the New Testament, the word for "appeared" is *opthe*. It is the root of our English words "optic," "optical," "optometry," and others that pertain to sight. The same word, *opthe,* is used in the story of the transfiguration of Jesus in Mark's Gospel, and its retelling in Matthew 17:1–8 and Luke 9:28–36. "Six days later Jesus took Peter, James, and John with him and led them up a high mountain where they were alone; and in their presence he was transfigured; his clothes became dazzling white, with a whiteness no bleacher on earth could equal. They saw Elijah appear, and Moses with him, and there they were, conversing with Jesus" (Mark 9:2–4 NEB). By his choice of words, St. Paul is indicating that his experience and those of the disciples were of the same kind, appearances.

Very close in meaning to the word "appeared" is the word "vision," used in the third account of St. Paul's conversion experience. According to Acts, when defending himself before King Agrippa, St. Paul said,

> On one such occasion I was traveling to Damascus with authority from the chief priests; and as I was on my way, Your Majesty, in the middle of the day I saw a light from the sky, more brilliant than the sun, shining all around me and my traveling-companions. We all fell to the ground, and then I heard a voice saying to me in the Jewish language, "Saul, Saul, why do you persecute me? It is hard for you, this kicking against the goad." I said, "Tell me, Lord, who are you"; and the Lord replied, "I am Jesus, whom you are persecuting. But now, rise to your feet and stand upright. I have appeared to you for a purpose: to appoint you my servant and witness, to testify both to what you have seen and to what you shall yet see of me." (Acts 26:12–17 NEB)

"And so, King Agrippa," Paul says, "I did not disobey the heavenly vision" (Acts 26:19 NEB).

We have no way of knowing if "vision" was St. Paul's choice of words, or if it was the choice of the author of the Acts. Either way, its use implies that the author of this book was comfortable with considering St. Paul's experience of the risen Christ to be a "vision." And the experiences of the disciples were no different.

Scholars have addressed the theological significance of visions. Marcus Borg and John Dominic Crossan suggest that, as visions, the resurrection appearances could not have been photographed.[1] They then point out that to call them "visions" does not belittle them. No one who has had a vision, they point out, would ever make light of it. That would certainly be true of St. Paul, whose entire life was disrupted and turned in a new

---

1. Borg and Crossan, *First Paul,* 150.

direction by his vision of Christ on the road to Damascus. Considering the resurrection appearances to be visions is biblical, and does not make them any less powerful and significant.

No matter if we are compelled to claim the physical, corporeal resurrection appearances to be literally true, or can accept the appearances of the risen Christ to be visions, we are considering historical events. It is both biblical and reasonable to determine that the resurrection appearances fall somewhere between being encounters with a corporeal, flesh-and-blood Jesus and an emotional experience that could be expressed: "I feel in my heart that Jesus is with me." The meaning lies between the crudely physical and the purely mystical. The visions experienced by the disciples and St. Paul were so real that they were of no doubt that the risen Christ was with them. The experience transformed them. They were changed, and the world was changed.

The change in the disciples is quite clear when looking at their behavior at the time of the crucifixion and soon after. When Jesus was arrested, the disciples ran for cover, to any hidey-hole they could find: "The disciples all deserted him and ran away" (Matt 26:56 NEB). At the crucifixion, it is just possible that some of them watched from a safe distance. "His friends had all been standing at a distance; the women who had accompanied him from Galilee stood with them and watched it all" (Luke 23:49 NEB). They were playing it safe.

St. Peter's activities were unique. "Peter followed him at a distance right into the High Priest's courtyard; and there he remained, sitting among the attendants, warming himself at the fire"(Mark 14:54 NEB). While there he denied three times that he knew Jesus. The final denial took place outside, on a porch. A maid saw him again and said to the bystanders, "'He is one of them'; and again, he denied it" (Mark 14:70 NEB).

Fear, desertion, denial, but very soon, a dramatic change. Peter and John, according to Acts, were bold enough to get themselves arrested. They were publicly proclaiming that Jesus had been raised from the dead, "They were still addressing the people when the chief priests came upon them . . . exasperated at their teaching the people and proclaiming the resurrection from the dead—the resurrection of Jesus. They were arrested and put in prison for the night" (Acts 4:1–3 NEB). Upon release, they continued to publicly profess their belief in Jesus, and were brought to court again. "They then called them in and ordered them to refrain from all public speaking and teaching in the name of Jesus" (Acts 4:18 NEB). Their response was,

"We cannot possibly give up speaking of things we have seen and heard" (Acts 4:20 NEB). They had been transformed. They were experiencing new life in themselves. Once cowards, they were now courageous. Something had happened to them, and something happened that changed the course of history. They explained it in three words, "He is risen." An overburdened metaphor. If anything may be considered a proof of the resurrection it is the transformation of the disciples, the birth of Christianity, and its spread throughout the world. That I, and you, and others are Christians these many years later attests to the continuous transforming power of the risen Christ.

Finally, there are two concepts of the resurrection, one small and one large. In the small concept, resurrection is thought of in terms of "What happens to me?" It becomes a promise of life after death on a purely individual basis. Any such idea of individual salvation would never have entered the minds of Jesus and his contemporaries. The covenants of the Old Testament were between God and Israel. Resurrection was something that would happen to everyone at the end of time. This understanding is expressed by Martha in her conversation with Jesus in the story of the raising of Lazarus. "Martha said to Jesus, 'If you had been here, sir, my brother would not have died. Even now I know that whatever you ask of God, God will grant you.' Jesus said, 'Your brother will rise again.' 'I know that he will rise again,' said Martha, 'at the resurrection on the last day'" (John 11:21–24 NEB). Martha knew nothing of an individual resurrection for her brother, and he was, after all, only resuscitated. Our individualistic views of life, death, and resurrection, supported by literal interpretations of the Bible, have trivialized the scope and significance of the resurrection.

An illustration of this trivialization is found in how some Christians approach church attendance. Their behavior is akin to making payments on a life insurance policy. "I will go to church now so that I can go to heaven then." The Christian faith is turned into something of a quid-pro-quo transaction with God. In contrast, the good news of the gospel is that our relationship with God is a gift that cannot and need not be earned.

In the large concept of the resurrection, God is making all things new. In this understanding, resurrection is not about me, not even about us: it is about all of creation. "Then he who sat on the throne said, 'Behold! I am making all things new!' (And he said to me, 'Write this down; for these words are trustworthy and true. Indeed, they are already fulfilled')" (Rev 21:5–6a NEB). Resurrection is about much more than survival after death and going to heaven. The resurrection, by the grace of God, is the point of transformation of the whole world. In Christ, God is recreating all things. God is remaking humanity, and as each of us has a part and place in humanity, we too are being made new. God is providing a new way of living, now, and by our relationships we move forward into that new life, now. John Shelby Spong put it this way: "one who has entered a relationship with God has entered the timelessness of God."[2] As God is eternal, it is an eternal relationship. That is resurrection.

2. Spong, *Resurrection*, 292.

The Empty Tomb

A PHYSICAL RESURRECTION ALL but demands an empty tomb. How can one person claim to have encountered a resuscitated Jesus in Galilee while another person is pointing to his body in a tomb in Jerusalem?

Though the tradition of the empty tomb is found in all four Gospels, in each the details are somewhat different. In Mark's Gospel (16:1–8) there are three women: Mary of Magdala, Mary the mother of James, and Salome. The stone sealing the tomb has already been rolled away. They are met by a youth in a white robe, who tells them that Jesus has been raised and has gone to Galilee. In Matthew's Gospel (28:1–7) there are only two women, Mary of Magdala and another unidentified Mary. They experience an earthquake and are met by an angel who rolls the stone away in their presence. Again, the women are told that Jesus has been raised from the dead and has gone to Galilee. In Luke's Gospel (24:1–11) there are several women, three of whom are later identified as Mary of Magdala, Joanna, and Mary the mother of James. They find the stone already rolled away, and are met by two men in dazzling garments. Nothing is said about Jesus going to Galilee, evidently because, at the end of this Gospel, Jesus instructs the disciples to stay in Jerusalem. In John's Gospel (20:1–2), Mary of Magdala is the only woman at the tomb, and she finds the stone already moved away. She runs to tell the disciples that the tomb is empty, and it is only after Peter and an unnamed disciple look into the tomb that she sees two angels in white. There is little consistency in these four accounts other than Mary of

Magdala being in all four, and the only constant is that the tomb is empty. It is interesting that the authorities accepted the story of the empty tomb. They went so far as to bribe the soldiers to say, "His disciples came by night and stole the body while we were asleep" (Matt 28:13 NEB).

The empty tomb stories seem to be a Jerusalem tradition while the appearance stories center on Galilee. In Mark's Gospel the women are told, "'He is going before you into Galilee; there you will see him, as he told you'" (Mark 16:7 NEB). Even in John's Gospel, in which the location of the earlier two appearances (chapter 20) seem to take place in Jerusalem, the next two appearances (chapter 21) take place in Galilee. Taking into consideration the announcements to the women in the first two Gospels, that Jesus had gone to Galilee, the Jerusalem appearances are a reverse of what is expected. The reverse in locations may be accounted for by accepting chapter 21 as an early addition to John's Gospel. The last two verses of chapter 20 have the character of an original ending for this Gospel. In the final analysis, we have an empty tomb tradition in Jerusalem and an appearance tradition in Galilee. These separate and independent traditions were combined at a very early date.

We have no witness to the actual resurrection, to what occurred in the tomb. The disciples did not know what had happened, and we cannot know. Even so, a positive conclusion may be drawn. The development of two separated and independent traditions, one of the appearances and another of the empty tomb, provide a stronger argument for the reality of the resurrection. A more full treatment of the tradition of the empty tomb can be found in Pannenberg, *Jesus—God and Man*.[1]

---

1. Pannenberg, *Jesus—God and Man*, 100.

9

Rescue or Relate

I DON'T BELIEVE THE purpose of Jesus' life was death. That is not the most creditable explanation of what Jesus did. It reduces the importance of his life to its last few hours.

The purpose of Jesus' life and death, and what he accomplished, is considered under the heading: the atonement. A way to clarify the meaning of this word is to break it down into its parts: "at-one-ment." There is a perception that things in this world are not as they should be, being at odds rather than at ease. In contrast, I offer the comment made of some persons: "They are comfortable in their own skin." Such persons, it can be said, "have gotten their act together," they are "at one with themselves." It appears that our world is not comfortable in its own skin. It is not at one with itself. We and our world are much in need of at-one-ment. We need to become more at one with ourselves, with one another, and with God.

The earliest followers of Jesus struggled to come to terms with the meaning of his life and death. It was only natural that, being Jewish, they would turn to their religious traditions and celebrations, and to the teachings of their prophets. The Jewish people deal with their lack of at-one-ment with God by means of the Day of Atonement, "*Yom Kippur.*" As described in the Old Testament book of Leviticus (chapter 16), animal sacrifices were a significant part of the observation of this day. A part of this observation that pertains to our understanding of the at-one-ment is that a goat was sent into the wilderness to bear away the sins of the people. This ritual of the sacrificial goat is the source of our idea of a scapegoat, a person or group made to bear the blame of others and to suffer the consequences in their place. An important passage from the prophets of the Old Testament is the "Servant Song" found in the prophet Isaiah. I quote only the concluding line: ". . . yet he bore the sin of many, and intercessions for the transgressors" (Isa 53:12 NRSV).

Do people today, as they look for meaning in life, give much thought to Jesus, to what he did or how he may have done it? It is easier to accept a brief, bumper-sticker–like slogan. Back, way back, in my teenage years, there were signs nailed to pine trees and fence posts on the outskirts of Baton Rouge that announced: "Only the Blood of Jesus Saves." During my high school years, I was active in our church youth group. I attended the Sunday evening meetings because the only alternative was to stay home and do homework. Also, I had good friends in the youth group. One of them had an old Jeep we ran around in. I can remember riding in it out into a swampy area to cut palms for Palm Sunday. My friend who owned the Jeep collected those "Only the Blood of Jesus Saves" signs. We kept our eyes open for them, and when one was spotted, he would pull it down and add it to his collection. As young Episcopalians we were put off by those signs without knowing why.

This anecdote about signs nailed up in the 1950s may seem old and dated, but Mel Gibson's 2004 movie *The Passion of Christ* is, in its own way, an "Only the Blood of Jesus Saves" sign. The movie was as off-putting as were those signs nailed to pine trees. The crucifixion of Jesus, any cruci-fixion, was terrible, cruel, barbaric, and bloody. Crucifixion is intended to be an awful way to die. Where the signs and the movie are misleading is that they give little thought to the life of Jesus. What he did, what he ac-complished, was the result of his life, and not only of his three hours on the cross and his death. In any consideration of what Jesus did, we must take into consideration the fullness of his life: actions, teachings, attitudes.

The historic creeds of the church are not helpful in guiding us to look at the full life of Jesus. In both the Nicene Creed and the Apostles' Creed we jump from the birth of Jesus to his death. In the Apostles' Creed we recite: "He was conceived by the power of the Holy Spirit and born of the Virgin Mary. He suffered under Pontius Pilate, was crucified, died, and was buried." It is as though we mention his birth only to be able to get to his death. Nothing is said about his life. It is ignored. We are deprived of the full story of what Jesus did and how he went about doing it. His compassion in healing the blind, lame, and diseased; his acceptance of the unacceptable shown in his willingness to share a meal with them; his parables that tell of a loving God—all need to be included.

And we need to move out of the past tense. It is a mistake to consider the at-one-ment a transaction that God executed and completed by Jesus' death on the cross. That does not take into consideration God's relationship with his creation before Jesus, or our responsibility in this relationship afterward. Historically, there was an event, the Jesus event, which occurred in a given place at a given time and that did initiate a new dynamic in our relationship with God. The significance of that event, however, is known only as its influence moves through time, through the years, into our lives. Our interest is not with an isolated historical event, but with the onset of a significant change in the dynamics of human existence. We are given a new way of relating to one another.

To move away from perceiving the at-one-ment as a once-upon-a-time rescue mission, a piece of business, and to find it a matter of relationships, I turn to St. Paul. He was unable to settle upon any one explanation of the at-one-ment. Throughout his letters, St. Paul wrote of Jesus' "sacrificial death." Also, he frequently used the word "reconciliation," as in 2 Corinthians 5:18 and Romans 5:10. This word, "reconciliation," the healing of relationships, offers a better approach for grappling with an understanding of the at-one-ment. "When anyone is united to Christ, there is a new world; the old order has gone, and a new order has already begun. From first to last this has been the work of God. He has reconciled us men to himself through Christ, and he has enlisted us in this service of reconciliation" (2 Cor 5:17–18 NEB). These two verses tie back into what was said earlier about the resurrection, that a "new world" is being created, being brought to life. In claiming that God "has reconciled us men to himself through Christ," St. Paul makes two points. First, the at-one-ment is God's doing; second, it is a matter of relationships. And, St. Paul keeps the dynamics of at-one-ment in this world by stating that "he has enlisted us in this service of reconciliation." At-one-ment is not our ticket into heaven when we die, but our guide for how to live here and now. Reconciliation with God cannot be separated from our reconciliation with one another as we live together in a world not at one with itself. Christianity is a very down-to-earth form of religion, using the common elements of water, bread, and wine in its rituals. It is concerned with our treatment of one another in our common day-to-day encounters. The Lord's Prayer, for example, is about the food we need, the debt we don't need, and forgiving one another here and now.

Reconciliation is an excellent synonym for at-one-ment because it places the concept within the dynamics of relationships. However, due to the centrality of the Lord's Supper, the Mass, the Eucharist, in Christian worship, it is impossible to avoid the images of sacrificial death and the blood of Jesus. Drawing upon the Book of Common Prayer of the Episcopal Church for examples, just before offering Holy Communion to the congregation, the priest says, "Christ our Passover is sacrificed for us." Then, in administering the wine, the priest says, "The Blood of Christ, the cup of salvation." I do not disparage the Holy Eucharist or question its place in Christian worship. Too frequently, though, the message of Easter, that Jesus overcame death, plays second fiddle to the message of Lent, that Jesus died a bloody sacrificial death. Easter is the good news of life overcoming death. The healing of the estranged relationship between God and humanity is achieved by the full life of Jesus in the constant attentiveness of God. God was in Christ, in his life and not just in his death. God was in Christ, all through his life, reconciling us to himself, restoring the relationship offered throughout all time. Reconciliation is a sound and biblical image of the dynamics of at-one-ment.

The dynamics of a continuous reconciliation is sketched for us in the parable of the nations in Matthew's Gospel. Before getting to the primary message of the parable there are a few issues that need clarification. In the opening verses of the parable (Matt 25:32–33 NEB), there is judgment and a separation of sheep from goats. To avoid being sidetracked by this separation, it is important to note that goats, too, are accepted into the love of God. Earlier in this Gospel, Jesus is recorded as having said, "It is not the healthy that need a doctor, but the sick" (9:12 NEB). If we can take the goats as representing the sick, those in need, Jesus is saying that he is primarily interested in the plight of the goats. It is also interesting to note that in the Exodus, when the Israelites were escaping from Egypt and instructed to mark their doors with blood so that the angel of death would pass over them, celebrated as the Passover, they were told the blood of a kid would do as well as that of a lamb. "You may take equally a sheep or a goat" (Exod 12:5b NEB). Goats are also God's creatures.

Now, consider the punishment described at the end of the parable of the nations: "The curse is upon you; go from my sight to the eternal fire that is ready for the devil and his angels" (Matt 25:41 NEB). That punishment would best be understood in light of most of the preceding parables. The parable of the wedding feast for the king's son (Matt 22:1–14 NEB) is a good example. "The kingdom of heaven is like this," Jesus said. A king was planning a wedding feast for his son, and he invited all the better folk, those in the social register. When the grill was hot and the "beasts" were slaughtered, he sent word that all was ready. All those he had invited ignored the invitation, and some even abused the king's servants who were sent to them. The king was furious, and he took his revenge. He sent his servants out again to drag in the street people, and dress them properly. No matter their lack of quality, or qualifications, they were invited and accepted. The party was on. The king then saw a man who was not dressed for a wedding. He was questioned by the king, but "he had nothing to say" for himself. The king said to his attendants, "Bind him hand and foot; turn him out into the dark, the place of wailing and grinding teeth" (Matt 22:14 NEB).

Jesus is not so harsh in his other parables, so why here? In refusing the free wedding garment, that stupid man was rejecting the full gift that was being offered. He was refusing to be clothed in grace. Perhaps, because he wanted to do it his way. It makes me think of Frank Sinatra's hit song with the refrain, "I did it my way." There are times when we cannot and should not demand our own way. The man in the parable could not accept his acceptance. He rejected the gift. The parable concludes, "for though many are invited, few are chosen." He refused being chosen. Only those who insist on being punished will be.

Returning to the primary message of the parable of the nations, "When the Son of Man comes . . . he will separate men into two groups . . . the sheep on his right hand and the goats on his left. Then the king will say to those on his right hand, 'You have my Father's blessing; come, enter and possess the kingdom that has been ready for you since the world was made. For when I was hungry, you gave me food; when thirsty, you gave me drink; when I was a stranger you took me into your home, when naked you clothed me; when I was ill you came to my help, when in prison you visited me'" (Matt 25:31–36 NEB). Those to whom he said this will reply, When in the world did we do any of that? "And the king will answer, 'I tell you this: anything you did for one of my brothers here, however humble, you did for me'" (Matt 25:40 NEB). As Jesus participated in God, we participate in Jesus, bringing reconciliation, at-one-ment. Care for our neighbor, without distinguishing sheep from goats, is the key.

Atonement is not about the next life, but about this life. It is not a rescue, fully accomplished once and for all. It is the first step in healing our relationships. Atonement is discovered and it is furthered in day-to-day relations, one person reaching to another with compassion. It flows on through human history by our willingness to be inclusive, caring, giving, and forgiving. Those traits overcome estrangement and separation and isolation by developing relationships. The world is made a better place, our lives more fulfilled, when we become one with one another and one with God. This is the fullness of atonement.

SIDEBAR

Atonement Theories

WITHIN THE TRADITIONS OF the church, there are numerous theories of how God in Christ brings about atonement. According to church teachings, Jesus atoned for our sins by his sacrificial death on the cross. Here, in no order of preference, are brief evaluations of the five most prominent theories of the atonement.

The victory theory holds that Jesus, in principle, defeated the powers of evil. According to this theory, by taking the very worst that Satan could throw at him, and living through it by means of his resurrection, Jesus broke the power of evil. There are problems. For one, the resurrection was not something Jesus accomplished on his own, but what God accomplished in and through him. It was not only Jesus' victory. Also, any casual observer would notice that evil is as rampant now as ever: terrorists, child molestation, torture, brutality, to mention only a few. Did Jesus break the powers of evil or only bend them a little? The explanation that he won the war, but various battles rage on, is of little consolation. If victory it was, it was only partial or only just begun, and that makes for an inadequate theory.

The moral theory begins with an acknowledgment that all behavior, good and bad, leads to consequences. So far, so good. Jesus, by taking upon himself the consequences of our dastardly behavior, set a moral example. The problem is that few of us heed advice, and an example is only somewhat better than advice. What we need is the willpower to do what we know we should and to avoid doing what we know we should not. Along those line, the church has always maintained that Jesus did change our circumstances, not just point us in a better direction by his good example.

The ransom theory does have the advantage of a biblical foundation. "For the Son of Man came not to be served but to serve, and to give his life as a ransom for many" (Mark 10:45 NEB). The idea of a ransom being paid can also be found in the Old Testament, but it is not supportive of the ransom theory of the atonement. "Truly, no ransom avails for one's life, there is no price one can give to God for it" (Ps 49:7 NRSV). The primary problem with this theory is the question, to whom is the ransom paid? A ransom is not paid to the parent of the abducted child, so God would not seem to be the likely recipient. If the ransom is paid to Satan, the implication is that Satan is more powerful than God, or at least powerful enough to make demands upon God. This cannot be so. Also, if there is such a creature as Satan (a subject considered earlier in chapter 2), he is a creature of God. As such, God could simply withdraw his creative and sustaining power and Satan would immediately cease to exist. Everything is held in existence by God. The ransom theory makes little sense because there is no reasonable recipient without degrading God.

The substitution theory goes something like this: We are so sinful, so totally depraved, that we deserve a horrible, painful death, and eternity in hell. Jesus loves us so much that he was willing to be substituted for us and to take upon himself the punishment we deserve. As wonderful as this makes Jesus, to that same extent it makes God awful. Can there be no forgiveness and acceptance, no atonement, until someone suffers? In the Lord's Prayer we ask that our debts, trespasses, sins be forgiven based on our willingness to forgive. We pray that we may forgive without extracting a payment or requiring a punishment. If we are expected to do so, cannot we expect as much from God? Is his ability to forgive, to offer reconciliation, limited? I do not think so. This theory makes God into a judgmental and cruel potentate.

The satisfaction theory is rooted in the Jewish sacrificial system and the rituals associated with the Day of Atonement. The place of blood sacrifice and the sacredness of blood is fundamental to this theory. At its core is the concept that God is so offended by human sin that propitiation is required to satisfy his righteousness. No finite being could do so much. Jesus, being human and divine, became the ultimate sacrifice. We have moved from the death of Jesus being a ransom, paid to we know not whom, to it being a debt paid to God to satisfy his righteousness. We are redeemed by the sacrifice, by the precious blood of Jesus. Except for the military, and first responders, to what extent do persons in this day find meaning in any kind of sacrifice? Even less is there any concept of the religious sacredness of blood. We have moved a long way, psychologically, culturally, and spiritually from the temple in Jerusalem and its sacrificial system. Also, this theory demeans God, making him something of a tit-for-tat bookkeeper who requires that any offense to his righteousness be balanced by someone being punished.

In one way or another, each of these theories of the atonement is flawed. Consequently, no one theory of the atonement has been fully adopted as the official doctrine of the church.

PART IV

God

10

Panentheism and Synergism

I DON'T BELIEVE IN the God we trust. For many, that God, inscribed on our money, has been replaced by the money itself. Who is now the God we trust? What has become of the God in whom we believed? A God in whom we can believe may be found by looking at the alternatives and engaging the mysteries. An alternative is an acceptance of panentheism. The mysteries are engaged under three headings: compassion, synergism, and vitality.

Belief in the existence of a god or gods is known as theism. In most cases there must be theism for there to be atheism; there must be something to refuse and reject. Rejection of the "God of the dollar bill" is rejection of the popular god of our culture. There is precedence for that rejection. The first Christians were accused of atheism because of their refusal to worship the popular gods of their culture. They rejected the state-supported gods as they held onto their Judeo-Christian monotheism. In consequence, those early Christians were persecuted as "nonbelievers," as "a-theists."

The accepted theism of our time is defective in two ways. The first is from an intrusion of materialism into our belief in God. One example of this intrusion is the prosperity gospel. The prosperity gospel teaches that financial blessings and material well-being are the will of God. This is a peculiar version of Christianity considering the itinerant nature of Jesus' life during his ministry. He is reported to have said, "Foxes have their holes, the birds their roosts; but the Son of Man has nowhere to lay his head" (Luke 9:58 NEB). The prosperity gospel proposes a way of following Jesus that, because of its materialism, is out of step with his life and his teachings. It can be considered a baptism of American materialism.

A second way in which theism has become misguided is by too strong a dependence on a transcendent image of God. This image is of a God outside our world, a God who engages with us from a supernatural position above us. From there, God intervenes miraculously, or fails to do so, in ways that are beyond our comprehension. A transcendent God can feel too distant and even too small. My descriptions of a God who is too small rest on the book *Your God Is Too Small*.[1] Images of a God too small are as prevalent and popular as they are misleading and inadequate.

One image of a God too small is the "Grand Puppet Master." In this image, God is an old man with a gray beard, controlling and manipulating everything. The problem with this image is that the Grand Puppet Master appears to have gotten the strings badly tangled. Too many aspects of creation are not working out well. If God is controlling everything, he is responsible for every good decision, for every happy day, for all love and joy. He is, though, equally responsible for every bad decision, for every painful and terrible disaster of every kind. This God is responsible for every tragic accident and illness, for every deadly shooting of every child in any neighborhood school, and for every terrorist attack on innocent civilians. Such a God is too small for the simple reason of his being incompetent or unloving. And a God who contradicts himself cannot still be God. To fall back on the glib explanation that God's ways are not our ways will not do. God's ways should be at least as good as our ways in our better moments. Blaming the devil has already been ruled out for reasons explained in chapter 2.

A second image of a God too small is "Mr. Fixit," with a cosmic tool belt around his waist. This image begs the question, "If God can fix it, why doesn't he?" Is God fickle, or just a bumbling meddler? This is the image of a primarily transcendent God who must be persuaded to intervene when life breaks down. That persuasion is most often thought to depend on our good behavior, correct beliefs, and copious prayers. But, by any of these means, can we manipulate God? Even for those who believe they have witnessed an intervention, a miracle, there is a problem. Why is one person "fixed," granted a miracle, while another person is not? A God who performs a miracle here, but not there, who fixes this, but not that, is too erratic to be trusted and worshiped.

1. Phillips, *Your God Is Too Small*, 15–30.

A third image of a God too small is the "Heavenly Bookkeeper," wearing a green, transparent visor and garters on his sleeves to keep them out of the ink. This is an image of a quiet and insidious God working behind the scenes, keeping score. It is the image of a God we sing of at Christmas in one of our popular carols. These objectionable words claim that Santa Claus is "making a list and checking it twice," obsessing over who has been "naughty" and who has been "nice." By implication, God is portrayed as a tit-for-tat bookkeeper, looking for our faults. Santa Claus should be a portrayal of God as a lover, not a scorekeeper. God is a lover who wishes for us to return his love, enter a relationship with him, to trust him. Relationships subjected to scorekeeping are damaged, even destroyed. Such a God is too small for being small minded.

A fourth image of a God too small is the "Tough Policeman," handcuffs at his belt. This concept encompasses all the legalistic images of God: judge, jury, and executioner. The weakness of this image is that too many despicable people live a life of leisure and die in comfort, while many genuinely good people live hard lives of suffering and loss, and die in misery. Has the jury been tampered with, or do we have a crooked judge? There is also the danger of the Tough Policeman becoming a moral policeman. Moral policemen exhibit an inclination to concentrate on the so-called "warm" sins, those that make one's palms sweat, such as drinking, gambling, dancing, sex. What are called "white-collar" sins, such as corruption, embezzlement, and abuse of power, are seldom considered. This moralistic God becomes too small when loving inclusion gives way to judgmental exclusion.

In my ministry, some years ago, before the world became as roiled as it now is, I became involved in a situation where an image of a "large" God was needed. A woman called me on the telephone, and I quickly realized she was very agitated. She was not someone who knew me, but had chosen to call an Episcopal church because her pastor was out of town and a member of her family was an Episcopalian. She told me that a friend had invited her to attend a service of devil worship. She thought it would be interesting and a bit of fun, so she accepted the invitation. To her dismay, she found herself among people who were deadly serious about their devil worship. The fear in her voice was palpable, even over the phone. It was almost possible to hear her shaking. I listened, tried to offer some assurance, and risked giving a few words of advice. As advice, I told her what she probably had already figured out for herself. I said to her, "Don't go back, do not ever go back. Stay away from those people." By way of assurance, what came to mind was part of a passage from the First Letter of John, "the one who is in you is greater than the one who is in the world" (1 John 4:4b NRSV). During a phone call with a distraught stranger is not the time for offering a theology of the devil. With those few words from the First Letter of John I tried to give her a mantra, of sorts, words proclaiming a God large enough to cover her fears. I also recommended that she speak to her own pastor when she could. I never heard from her again and can only hope she found a God large enough to dispel her fear.

Considering the vastness of the cosmos, even the size of our galaxy, we need a correspondingly "large" God. The image we need is of a God large enough to encompass and embrace all, while not losing touch with us. A version of theism that provides an image of such a God is panentheism. The meaning of the word "panentheism" becomes more clear when it is read backwards: "theism," the Greek word for believing in God; "en," meaning in; "pan," meaning all or everything.[2] Panentheism is a long word for God being always everywhere in creation.

Panentheism was the version of theism generally accepted in Celtic Christianity, and I first encountered the concept in *Listening to the Heartbeat of God*, a book on Celtic spirituality.[3] Celtic Christianity has an important place in the history of the Church of England and in the Episcopal Church in this country. Christianity reached the British Isles at an early and unknown date. It is known to have been there by the year 209 CE, the recorded date of the martyrdom of St. Alban. Christianity in the British Isles probably arrived from two sources, trade with Christian communities around the Mediterranean and Christians in the Roman army. Due to the growing weakness of Rome, and its fall in 467 CE, Christianity in the British Isles was cut adrift and left to develop on its own for hundreds of years. Celtic Christianity is a unique form of the Christian faith that lasted until the Synod of Whitby in 664, at which time it submitted to the authority of the church in Rome.

The influence of Celtic spirituality, however, has not been lost, as evidenced in the writings of John Scotus Eriugena, a philosopher of the ninth century. J. Philip Newell makes the claim that Eriugena was the greatest teacher produced by Celtic Christianity. He taught that God is not "all things," which would be pantheism, but "in all things," which is panentheism.

---

2. Borg, *Heart of Christianity*, 66.

3. Newell, *Listening to the Heartbeat of God*, 38.

God's presence in all things led Eriugena to believe in the essential goodness of creation.

An acceptance of panentheism shows up in John Macquarrie's *Principles of Christian Theology*. What is found there is the statement that though God is wholly distinct from the world, he is present and manifest throughout the world. This, Macquarrie claims, is an expression of panentheism and a guard against exaggerated transcendence.[4] The mystery of God's relation to his creation, how he fills the world without "living" in the world, is more easily understood from the point of view of panentheism and its image of an immanent God than from traditional theism.

Panentheistic images of God are found throughout the Bible. In Acts there is a statement attributed to St. Paul that is panentheistic: "Then Paul stood before the Court of Areopagus and said: 'Men of Athens, I see that in everything that concerns religion you are uncommonly scrupulous'" (Acts 17:22 NEB). St. Paul then says he believes them to be scrupulous because he has noticed an altar bearing the inscription, "To an Unknown God." He says, "What you worship but do not know—this is what I now proclaim" (Acts 17:23 NEB). St Paul then proceeds to say, God "is not far from each one of us, for in him we live and move, in him we exist" (Acts 17:27b–28a NEB). Though expressed in the reverse—we in God rather than God in the world—what St. Paul was saying is clearly panentheistic in the sense of God's immanence, and his interaction with us.

Those words, attributed to St. Paul, are paraphrased in the service of Holy Communion in the Episcopal Church, in the blessing of the bread and wine: "All this we ask through your Son Jesus Christ. By him, and with him, and in him, in the unity of the Holy Spirit all honor and glory is yours, Almighty Father, now and forever."[5] We have here a declaration in the worship of the church that we live by, with, and in a relationship with God. Our images of God need not put him out there, somewhere, magnificently transcendent. He is with us, beside us, all around us, here. We are within his embrace even when we do not know it.

We move now from the alternate image provided by panentheism to the mysteries. The three mysteries I associate with the nature of a God large enough for our time are: compassion, synergy, and vitality. I choose "mystery" rather than "attribute" because the nature of God will always be a mystery to us. There are two basic types of mystery, the mystery to

---

4. Macquarrie, *Principles of Christian Theology*, 120.

5. Episcopal Church, *Book of Common Prayer*, 363.

be solved and the mystery of a person. In a mystery to be solved, like the typical "whodunit," once we identify the culprit or discover the answer, we move on. The mystery of a person is quite different, for the better we get to know a person, the deeper the mystery becomes. We become aware of the depth of the person, and the limit of our knowledge of him or her. It is in this second sense that mystery is applied to our understanding of God.

Of the three mysteries of God previously mentioned, I begin with compassion. David Felton and Jeff Procter-Murphy point out that "For the Jew, compassion is the secret name for God."[6] Looking at the compassion of God as it is expressed in the Old Testament, the Holiness Code in the book of Leviticus provides a starting place. In what may be called a socioeconomic passage, compassion for the poor is presented as a legal statue. "When you reap the harvest of your land, you shall not reap right into the edges of your field; neither shall you glean the loose ears of your crop; you shall not completely strip your vineyard nor glean the fallen grapes. You shall leave them for the poor and the alien. I am the Lord your God" (Lev 19:9–10 NEB). God is forever concerned for the marginalized and downtrodden.

The God of compassion is also the God of justice. According to Marcus Borg, justice is the social expression of compassion.[7] The merging of compassion and justice is clear in the prophets of the Old Testament, who cry out for justice in the name of God. "But let justice roll down like waters, and righteousness like an ever-flowing stream" (Amos 5:24 NRSV). "He has told you, O mortal, what is good; and what does the Lord require of you but to do justice, and to love kindness, and to walk humbly with your God" (Mic 6:8 NRSV). "Learn to do good, seek justice, rescue the oppressed, defend the orphan, plead for the widow" (Isa 1:17 NRSV). It is clear in the prophets that justice, compassion, and a strong desire to alleviate suffering flow from the character of God.

The Psalms are equally expressive of God's compassion. "Thou, Lord, art God, compassionate and gracious, forbearing, ever constant and true" (Ps 86:16 NEB). "He has won a name by his marvelous deeds; the Lord is gracious and compassionate" (Ps 111:4 NEB). "The Lord is gracious and compassionate, forbearing, and constant in his love" (Ps 145:8 NEB).

Moving on to the New Testament, God's constant love is clearly stated: "God is love; he who dwells in love is dwelling in God, and God in him"

---

6. Felton and Procter-Murphy, *Living the Questions*, 205.

7. Borg, *Heart of Christianity*, 200.

(1 John 4:16b NEB). "Dear friends, let us love one another, because love is from God. Everyone who loves is a child of God and knows God, but the unloving know nothing of God. For God is love" (1 John 4:7–9a NEB). "God is love" does not describe a static condition, but the active nature of God. Paramount in expressions of love are empathy and compassion, the ability to feel another's feelings and the will to act upon what is felt. Love is not a shallow sentiment, but a motivation at the core of personhood. This is true of the person of God and of our own personhood. All of the passages, from the Old Testament and the New Testament, offered as illustrations of the compassion of God, are summed up in these words of Jesus found in Luke's Gospel: "Be compassionate as your Father is compassionate" (Luke 6:36 NEB). Compassion is a piece of the mystery of God's relation to his creation.

Second among the mysteries of God to be considered is the synergistic aspect of his activity. At its most simple, synergism is a joint action. Synergism is the interaction of two elements that, when combined, produce an effect greater than the two simply added together. It is not necessary that the parties in a synergistic relationship be equal. The synergistic aspect of God's relationship with us is strong evidence of his immanence and of his acceptance of us as important to his creation.

The creation myth in the book of Genesis contains stories that are open to synergistic interpretation. God created a garden and creatures to inhabit the garden. Man cooperated by working the land and naming the creatures. "Then the Lord God planted a garden in Eden away to the East, and there he put the man whom he had formed" (Gen 2:8 NEB). "The Lord God took the man and put him in the garden of Eden to till it and care for it" (Gen 2:15 NEB). "Then the Lord God said 'It is not good for the man to be alone. I will provide a partner for him.' So God formed out of the ground all the wild animals and all the birds of heaven. He brought them to the man to see what he would call them, and whatever the man called each living creature, that was its name" (Gen 2:18–19 NEB). These verses are more clearly synergistic when understood as part of a creation myth. They are theology rather than history. A purely historical interpretation locks them in time, as a singular, isolated cooperation. Read as religious myth, these stories indicate the ongoing relationship between God and humans as co-workers, even if unequal in creative powers.

A second biblical illustration of a synergistic relationship is that of God and Moses found in the book of Exodus. Throughout the story of the exodus, we find a cooperative relationship between God and Moses. From the banks of the River Nile to the promised land on the other side of the Jordan River, the two work together. It is not at all extreme to consider that joint venture a synergistic relationship.

Before addressing the synergistic nature of the Exodus, it is necessary to explain that the account is not objectively historical. Walter Brueggemann points out that those who pieced together the storyline of the Exodus, Israel's escape from slavery in Egypt, approached it as liturgical rather than historical. He finds reasons for this interpretation in that the Exodus passage is an instruction on how the Passover is to be reenacted and celebrated.[8] This section begins, "These are the rules for the Passover" (Exod 12:43b NEB). Earlier in chapter 12, there are other indications that this material was assembled for religious purposes. "You shall keep this day as a day of remembrance, and make it a pilgrimage, a festival of the Lord; you shall keep it generation after generation as a rule for all time" (Exod 12:14 NEB). The celebration of Passover observes these rules even to this day.

Moving on with the synergistic elements, the exodus story begins with the enslaved Israelites crying out to God. This storyline can be picked up with God speaking to Moses from a burning bush that is not being consumed by the flames: "The Lord said, 'I have indeed seen the misery of my people in Egypt" (Exod 3:7 NEB). Moses is then enlisted by God to work with him, "Come now; I will send you to Pharaoh and you shall bring my people Israel out of Egypt" (Exod 3:10 NEB). Moses is to represent God; he is to convince the Israelites that he does truly speak for their God and convince Pharaoh to free them. While Moses is arguing with Pharaoh, God is performing signs and miracles to show his presence, involvement, and power. These signs culminate in God inflicting ten plagues on the Egyptians. The tenth plague brings about the release of the Israelites. God informed the Israelites, "On that night I shall pass through the land of Egypt and kill every first-born of man and beast" (Exod 12:17 NEB). But, as instructed, the Israelites marked their doors with the blood of a lamb, and their firstborn were spared, passed over. Because of this horrific plague, Pharaoh capitulates: "Go and worship the Lord, as you ask; take your sheep and cattle and go; and ask God's blessing on me also" (Exod 12:32 NEB). The Egyptians relent, and Moses leads the Israelites as they flee from Egypt. This is celebrated as Passover.

There are two things of interest in this account: God's despicable killing of innocent children is overlooked, and the telling is rubrical rather

8. Brueggemann, *Introduction to the Old Testament*, 57.

than historical. Rubrics are directions for the conduct of a service of worship. What we have here is not directly about the Passover event, but about the observance of Passover. This is made clear in the following verse: "Then, when your children ask you, 'What is the meaning of this rite?' you shall say, 'It is the Lord's Passover, for he passed over the houses of the Israelites in Egypt when he struck the Egyptians but spared our houses'" (Exod 12:26 NEB). This passage is explanatory, and not an historical account. Throughout the story of the exodus, even where it is not historical, it describes a cooperative effort of God and Moses, from the escape from Egypt, through the wilderness of Sinai, to the promised land. It is not too extreme to consider that joint venture a synergistic relationship.

Turning to the New Testament, St. Paul implies an aspect of synergism in his Letter to the Philippians. "Friends, I want you to understand that the work of the gospel has been helped on, rather than hindered, by this business of mine" (Phil 1:12 NEB). St. Paul appears to be saying that God's presence in Jesus, and his, Paul's, efforts, are succeeding because they have been working together. There is an organic image of synergism in John's Gospel where Jesus is reported to have said, "I am the vine, and you are the branches. He who dwells in me, as I dwell in him, bears much fruit; apart from me you can do nothing" (John 15:5 NEB).

This passage from the Gospel according to John segues easily into a quote attributed to St. Augustine of Hippo: "Without God, we cannot. Without us, God will not." This statement, from one of the most influential fathers of the church, is of a cooperation that can qualify as synergism. We have now a second piece of the mystery of God's relation to his creation.

Third among the mysteries of God is his vitality. John Macquarrie wrote, "An inert, static being could hardly be called 'God.'"[9] Within the Christian church, there is broad acceptance of a definition of God as "Being," not a being or even the being but being itself. God is elemental, fundamental being. The highly regarded theologian Paul Tillich defined God as the "Ground of Being." This definition never intended to describe God as static and affirms that the ground of everything that is, is living creativity.[10] God can just as well be described as "Animating Being." God is the energy that brings all else into being. God is the vitality, the life force, of creation.

In both the Old and New Testaments of the Bible, there are passages that speak of God as a dynamic "life force." The creation myth offers an

9. Macquarrie, *Principles of Christian Theology*, 216.
10. Tillich, *Courage to Be*, 33.

early illustration. "Then the Lord God formed a man from the dust of the ground and breathed into his nostrils the breath of life" (Gen 2:7 NEB). This is an obvious image of animation. It is a mistake, though, to consider this a singular event that took place in ancient history. It was not a lone, unusual example of the activity of God. And it should not be thought of only in the past tense. The book of Genesis is not about what "was," but about what "is." The first half of the book of Genesis is best understood as an explanation of our relationship with God in the here and now. A comment that supports the claim just made is that God is not the "Great I Was," but the "Great I Am." In *Living the Questions*, David Felton and Jeff Procter-Murphy give credit for this comment on God's presence to the twentieth-century Quaker mystic, Rufus Jones.[11]

A way of seeing the vital presence of God is to realize that he is not just in the big bang, but in all the sparks still flying about. In *The Principles of Christian Theology*, John Macquarrie quotes the Danish philosopher Soren Kierkegaard as having seen that God "becomes the third party in every relationship of love."[12] Loving relationships become the homes of those sparks.

A passage in the New Testament that illustrates the dynamic nature of God reaches back into the creation myth in the book of Genesis. This passage is found in the prologue to John's Gospel, "The Word, then, was with God at the beginning, and through him all things came to be; no single thing was created without him. All that came to be was alive with his life, and that life was the light of men. The light shines on in the dark, and the darkness has never mastered it" (John 1:2–5 NEB). Other translations of this passage offer interesting insights. "The light shines in the darkness, and the darkness did not overcome it" (NRSV). "And the light shineth in darkness; and the darkness comprehended it not" (KJV).

The author of the Gospel according to John has drawn upon the Zoroastrian religion of ancient Persia, in which the belief was held that in creation there are two opposing powers, the god of light (Ahriman) and the God of darkness (Ormuzd). All of creation was thought to be caught up in this battle between light and dark, good and evil, and every person must choose a side. In John's Gospel, the Word of God, Jesus, entered this mythological world, creating a field of force as light and life. In Jesus, the life force of God was so strong that the powers of darkness could not even comprehend it, much less overcome it.

11. Felton and Procter-Murphy, *Living the Questions*, 224.

12. Kierkegaard, *Works of Love*, in Macquarrie, *Principles of Christian Theology*, 350.

The final passage chosen to identify God as the "life force" of creation is at the very end of the Bible. "Then he who sat on the throne said, 'Behold! I am making all things new!'" (Rev 21:5 NEB). All of creation is being transformed, transfigured, being made new by God. According to this passage, and the full message of the New Testament, God's intention is not to evacuate the world, but to renew it. The so-called theology of the rapture is unbiblical and badly mistaken. The rapture is a belief that when this world comes to an end the righteous will be "beamed up" while the unrighteous will be left behind to suffer the calamities of the end times. God's unfathomed energy is everywhere, and at all times working to redeem his creation, not destroy it. Considering what is here said about God as a dynamic life force, an admittedly extreme metaphor could be: God is primal energy with compassion.

The biblical passages above, from the book of Genesis, from John's Gospel, and from the Revelation of John, support an image of God as Animating Being, a vivifying life force. These passages support this third piece in the mystery of God's interaction with his creation. He is a God of life, yet larger than life, encompassing and energizing all that is.

An image of a God we can trust emerges, a God who is for us compassionately, with us synergistically, animating us by his life force. This panentheistic God is inescapably expressed in Psalm 139:

> Where can I go from your spirit? Or where can I flee from your presence? If I ascend to heaven, you are there; if I make my bed in Sheol, you are there. If I take the wings of the morning and settle at the farthest limits of the sea even there your hand shall lead me, and your right hand shall hold me fast. (Ps 139:7–10 NRSV)

God is in the world, yet more, with us as well as beyond us, mysteriously known and unknown, a compassionately synergistic life force.

SIDEBAR

God's Name

ANY STUDY OF THE name of God will lead to the Kenite theory. This theory proposes that an obscure clan of the Midianites, the Kenites, had an influence on the Hebrew religion, and specifically on the name given to God.[1]

The Kenites are mentioned in the book of Judges (1:16), and in 1 Chronicles (2:25), but the most significant passage for our purposes is found in the story of Moses and the burning bush in the book of Exodus. The storyline begins at 2:11. Moses, when a grown man, saw an Egyptian beating a Hebrew. He killed the Egyptian and hid the body. The next day, Moses finds that others know what he has done. He flees from Egypt to escape punishment and settles in Midian. In Midian, Moses encounters the daughters of Reuel, the priest of Midian, and defends them from shepherds who are preventing them from watering their flock. As a result, he is accepted by Reuel, goes to work for him, and marries one of his daughters, Zipporah. As a result of his marriage, Moses becomes a member of the family of the priest of Midian. Interestingly, the name of Moses's father-in-law has now become Jethro.

While Moses is tending his father-in-law's flock in the wilderness at Mount Horeb, "There the angel of the Lord appeared to him in the flame of a burning bush. Moses noticed that, although the bush was on fire, it was not being burnt up" (Exod 3:2 NEB). "When the Lord saw that Moses had

---

1. Cross and Livingston, eds., *Oxford Dictionary of the Christian Church*, s.v. "Kenites."

turned aside to look, he called to him out of the bush" (Exod 3:4 NEB). Moses is told to come no closer, and to take off his sandals because he is on holy ground. Then he is told, "I am the God of your forefathers, the God of Abraham, the God of Isaac, the God of Jacob" (Exod 3:6a NEB). God has seen the affliction of his people and heard their cry.

"Come now," God says to Moses, "I will send you to Pharaoh and you shall bring my people Israel out of Egypt" (Exod 3:10 NEB). Moses has a number of problems. The one at issue here is that he does not know this God's name. "Then Moses said to God, 'If I go to the Israelites and tell them that the God of their forefathers has sent me to them, and they ask me his name, what shall I say?'" (Exod 3:13 NEB). "God answered, 'I AM; that is who I AM. Tell them that I AM has sent you to them'" (Exod 3:14 NEB). God's answer is a problem. First, "I AM" is a form of the verb "to be." God's name is a verb rather than a noun. And God's answer can also be translated, "I will be what I will be." God will not be pinned down and controlled by the use of his name. God's essence is dynamic, pure activity. God is a verb.

A second problem is that in Hebrew "I AM" is written in four consonants, YHWH, known as the tetragrammaton. Early Hebrew was written without vowels. Consequently, no one knows for certain what the correct spelling is. The best biblical scholarship teaches that the name of God is "YAHWEH." This problem is even more complex because the name of God was never spoken. The name of God was too sacred to be spoken, so the word for lord, *adonai*, was used instead.

Between the sixth and tenth centuries CE, Hebrew grammarians known as the Massoretes[2] worked on the Hebrew text, adding vowels in the form of "pointings," small markings to represent the vowels and establish correct pronunciation. When they came to the name of God, which would have been written YHWH, they inserted the vowels for *adonai*, to guide the reader away from speaking the sacred name of God. Through a mistake, the vowels from *adonai* and the four consonants YHWH were combined to produce the hybrid nonword "YeHoWaH." The Y became a J and the W a V due to the different alphabets used in various languages, giving us Jehovah as the name of God. By popular use, Jehovah has become an acceptable name for God.

However, according to the book of Genesis, the Hebrew people knew the name of God from the beginning. "It was then that people began using

2. Cross and Livingston, eds., *Oxford Dictionary of the Christian Church*, s.v. "Massoretes."

the Lord's Holy name in worship" (Gen 4:26b GN). The story in the book of Exodus, of a God whose name is not known, introduces a different tradition of God, a tradition with Kenite influence, and the name is "YAHWEH."

11

Power and Knowledge

I DON'T BELIEVE GOD is in complete control. That statement appears to contradict the belief that God is all-powerful. However, it is not necessarily so that an all-powerful God must also be completely controlling.

God is not fully known to us, and that is always a good place to begin. One theological position declares that not enough is known about God for any positive statement to be made. Only the negative can be stated. We can only say what God is not. This theological position is given the name "*via negativa*," the negative way. We may, though, make a few assumptions about God, so long as we handle them loosely and make no definitive claims.

The assumptions about the nature and character of God are called his attributes. So long as they are not accepted and taught as iron-clad truths beyond question, they serve us well. They are what we think God ought to be, what we want him to be and need him to be. They are projections onto God of what we think is best for us in our relationship with him. The selected attributes that are under consideration here are: omnipotence, his being all-powerful; omniscience, his being all-knowing; immutability, his being unchanging; omnipresence, his being all-present; and loving, that he is love. The first four of these attributes are not biblical, and each is a bit flawed. The fifth is biblical but needs clarification. All are images of God expressed metaphorically.

THE ATTRIBUTES OF GOD

God is Love

The love of God for his creation is the guiding influence behind all the attributes, and particularly so in God's utilization of his power. Drawing briefly on the previous chapter, the words "God is Love" do not describe a static condition, but the active nature of God. God is not known objectively but known by what he does in his relation to his creation.

In the Old Testament, the Hebrew word for "love" that is most expressive of God's love is "*hesed*." This word means more than our English word "love," and the two words, "*hesed*" and "love," are not synonymous. The Hebrew *hesed* is often translated into English as "steadfast-love" (Ps 1 18:1 NRSV and Hos 2:19 NRSV). It has also been translated into English as "loving-kindness," as "loving-mercy," and as "enduring steadfast love." *Hesed* speaks to the persistence, even perseverance, of God's love for his people. In the Old Testament, God's love is directed toward his covenant people, Israel, rather than to any individual. Even so, God demonstrated the mercy and steadfastness of his love.

When we turn to the New Testament for our understanding of love, we encounter an interesting situation. The Greek language in which the New Testament was written has different words for different kinds of love. In English, we have only the one word "love" to express its various and many subtleties of meaning. There is only the one word, in English, to express a love of music, of chocolate, a love of spouse and children, of country. And no man would dare suggest that his love for football is the same as his love for his wife—certainly not in her presence. No matter the circumstances, there is only one word to use, putting pressure on that man's command of adjectives and adverbs. On the other hand, the Greek language has different words for different forms of love: *eros*, that comes into English as erotic, sexual love; *philia*, which comes to us as social love, friendship; and *storge*, family affection. The word for love most often used in the New Testament is *agape*. For example, *agape* is used in this often-quoted verse: "God loved the world so much that he gave his only Son, that everyone who has faith in him may not die but have eternal life" (John 3:16 NEB). *Agape* refers to the will rather than to the emotions. It is a matter of choice more than a romantic feeling. The clearest indication of God's love for us is revealed in the life of Jesus, in how he lived his life and in what he said and did. He chose never to turn any person away. Again and again, in his compassion for others he manifested a God of love.

Jesus manifested a loving God, not a controlling God. The nature of love is that it cannot be controlling. This is so for the simple reason that control destroys love. An illustration of the destructive force of control is found in its effect upon marriage. Recently, I joined my two sisters in New Orleans to celebrate the birthday of the youngest. She is a successful marriage and family therapist. We resumed an ongoing discussion of family relationships. What I learned in that discussion is that there is a power struggle, to some degree, in every marriage. It is a struggle, my therapist sister tells me, that neither husband nor wife should fight to win. The loser will become very unhappy, and the marriage will never again be the same, or as good. The relationship will be seriously damaged. To quote my sister, "You can be a winner, or you can be married." The power and control, the decision-making, in any healthy relationship must flow back and forth between husband and wife from situation to situation. It is also found that the one with the weakest ego will fight the hardest to win. Love does not, cannot seek control. A loving God will not be a controlling God.

God is All-Powerful

A doctrine of God that posits an omnipotent, all-powerful God is not contradicted by maintaining that God chooses not to be all-controlling. God can exercise his power in a more circumspect manner. Being all-powerful does not require that he be in full control of every minute detail in every individual's life. We are in the hands of a lover, not a control freak. Looking back to the previous chapter, God is not the Grand Puppeteer, but the Grand Lover. God does not have his way by manipulation, coercion, or any arbitrary exercise of power. Divine love takes precedence over divine power.

That love takes precedence even over authority is illustrated in the life of Jesus. "They came to Capernaum, and on the Sabbath he went to the synagogue and began to teach. The people were astounded at his teaching, for unlike the doctors of the law, he taught with a note of authority" (Mark 1:21–22 NEB). Then, though it was the Sabbath, he healed a man (Mark 1:25–26 NEB). The doctors of the law were custodians of the traditional interpretations of Scripture and opposed healing on the Sabbath. They quoted from prooftexts and prior teachings. Jesus spoke on his own authority, without counsel or limitations, and without imposing his teachings on his audience. His parables are a clear example of his style of teaching and his use of authority. By their very nature, his parables were open to a variety of responses. They were not arbitrary, nor did they attempt to control those being told the parable. Jesus was decisive without being peremptory.

Jesus' parables exercise a different form of authority. They are invitational. They invite us to find ourselves within the story, to respond, to decide what the parable may mean for us in our own life. We are also free to decide that the parable does not apply to us in any way and reject it outright. The choice of response is ours. The well-known parable of the good Samaritan ends with a question, "Which, of these three do you think was neighbour to the man who fell into the hands of robbers?" (Luke 10:29–37 NEB). The three are a priest and a Levite, both of whom passed by on the other side of the road, and a Samaritan. There was no love lost between Israelites and Samaritans. By extension, the issue becomes, "Under circumstances similar to those in the parable, what would I do?" It is my choice. Jesus did not use his parables as blunt instruments, but as encouragement for self-reflection. The parables may be taken to indicate that the God revealed by Jesus does not pummel the world. He lures it.

By his attractiveness, God lures the world into following him. We are always free to not take the lure. His use of power is persuasive rather than coercive. An all-powerful God who chooses to get his way by being attractive is very subtle, just as what attracts one person to another is a subtle mystery. That mystery became the center of conversation on a late-night television show I watched many years ago. I cannot remember who the host of the show was, or many of the details. Kirk Douglas was the guest, and I do remember that he was asked what made a woman attractive to him. His answer was that a woman who found him attractive was attractive to him. That kind of mutual attraction makes sense. By analogy, Kirk Douglas's answer could indicate that a God who finds us attractive enough to love us would be attractive to us. It is by attractiveness rather than by pushiness that God gets his way with us. Taking a thought from Robert Farrar Capon, God romances creation.[1] He draws creation to himself by romancing it. And romance is the beginning of a relationship.

We are free to respond to God's attractiveness, free to enter the relationship offered, and equally free to reject it. Basic to the Christian understanding of human nature is that we have freedom of choice. This concept of freedom is rooted in the creation of humans in the image of God, as told

1. Capon, *Romance of the Word*, 202.

in the creation myth in the early chapters of the book of Genesis, "So God created man in his own image; in the image of God he created him; male and female he created them" (Gen 1:27 NEB). Our creation in the image of God means that we share, to a limited extent, in God's sovereignty and responsibility for the world, and that we have a finite degree of freedom and creativity. As manifested in the life of Jesus, God does not strong-arm us, but attracts and persuades us. God has relinquished his control over us. And God takes the risk that his will may not always be done. Our freedom of choice is implied throughout the Bible, Old Testament and New Testament. The importance of how we choose to use this freedom is expressed starkly in the book of Deuteronomy: "Today I offer you the choice of life and good, or death and evil. . . . I offer you the choice of life or death, blessing or curse. Choose life and then you and your descendants will live" (Deut 30:15–19 NEB). A dog has no choice but to be a dog. We, though, may choose to be a cur, to fight over every bone, and die before our death, or we may choose to be here for others, and live in their hearts long after our death.

God is All-Knowing

The freedom we have impinges upon God's ability to be all-knowing, omniscient. Ellen F. Davis quotes a rabbinic commentator as observing that "God can only know things that can be known."[2] Our freedom is a limiting factor in what God can know. When we face a situation in which we must make a choice, the outcome cannot be known because there is no outcome until we decide and act. By our decision, and the action we take, we bring something into existence that had no existence before. What does not exist cannot be known; there is nothing to be known.

An example can be found in the book of Genesis, in the creation myth. Eve took a piece of forbidden fruit and shared it with Adam. Their eyes were opened, they were enlightened and became aware of their true nature. Then they realized that they were naked. They heard the Lord God approaching and they hid from him. "But the Lord God called to the man and said to him. 'Where are you?'" (Gen 3:9 NEB). A good interpretation of this part of the story begins by disregarding the possibility that God wanted to know what fig tree they were hiding behind. The important thing God wanted to know was, "Where are you in relation to me? Now that you have

2. Davis, *Getting Involved with God*, 59.

done this thing I asked you not to do, where are we in our relationship with each other?" Even now, that is the question. Where are we in relation to God? It is difficult for him to know because we are still hiding from him. Not until we choose and act do we bring an outcome into existence. What does not exist is not there to be known, even by God. God can only know what is knowable.

God's knowledge is restricted by the broad freedoms he has granted. Freedom of choice is not an aspect of human nature that is isolated from and independent of the world that surrounds us. Our freedom is part of, dependent upon, a general and pervasive freedom that permeates creation. This is not to say that our freedom is a cause of this general freedom. A casual observation reveals that hurricanes are free to blow, forest fires are free to burn, cancer cells are free to grow, pandemics are free to develop, and sharks are free to feed along popular beaches. God does not specifically call any of this into being, nor does he cancel any of it out. To curb any of this great and terrifying freedom would be to limit human freedom.

Even a small rock has its own kind of passive freedom. A small boy, attracted to that small rock, is free to choose it as a pet rock, put it into his pocket and take it home to add to his collection of valuables. That same small boy is also free to take up that small rock and fling it through the front window of the nearest house. If the freedom of that small rock were to be somehow "fixed," preventing it from becoming a projectile, to that same extent the freedom of that small boy to enjoy seeing and hearing glass shatter would be limited. He would be deprived of the freedom to make a mischief. As well, there would be a limit to the mischief humans are free to inflict upon one another, and there is little evidence of such a limit. But, for humans to be able to exercise their God-given freedom, freedom must be deeply and broadly a basic aspect of creation.

God is Unchanging

The immutability of God, that he is unchangeable, is another attribute that should be examined and clarified. Christianity is a matter of relationships, with God and with one another. In any relationship, each party to the relationship is affected by the other. A panentheistic God, in the world, would be affecting the world and, as well, would be affected by the world. Process theology holds this to be true. David Felton and Jeff Procter-Murphy express their acceptance of process theology by asserting that God himself is in process, constantly changing and evolving with us.[3] God is not static. How God may change, and still be a God of sufficient stability for Christians to depend upon, is expressed in the concept of "faithfulness." God is always faithful to himself, neither erratic nor inconsistent, always true to himself. God is, also, always faithful to us, though in a relationship constantly in flux, in transition, in a state of unrest that affects all parties to the relationship.

God is All-Present

The final attribute to be considered here is God's omnipresence, the belief that God is with us always and everywhere. It may be said that to be present with us in a world that is constantly changing, God must, so to speak, "go with the flow." His presence rides on his faithful flexibility, his presence in our every up and every down, in every situation, be it good or bad. This is not an interventionist God who steps in sporadically to bail us out of a bad situation. The belief in a God who intervenes, from time to time, appears clouded by his failure to intervene in so many dire situations. God does not work so much through intervention as through constant presence. This immanent God must be more than a mystical presence diffused throughout space like the light of day, and not, so far as we know, as dark matter. We have in God a constant loving presence rather than an intermittent involvement.

It is a mistake to seek a loving God in magical appearances. He should be sought in relational situations. Rather than look for him to do something occasionally, we should look for him to be here constantly, not tampering with the outcome, not with "his thumb on the scale," just lovingly here. An old saying goes something like this: "Don't just stand there, do something!" In pastoral care, just the reverse is often all that is possible. "Don't do anything, just be there." In the face of tragedy and death, seldom can anything be done, seldom can anything be said, to make things better. Getting to the bereaved, being there, is what is all important.

Church women everywhere intuitively know this to be so. They set out with their casserole dishes to be with those who are troubled and hurting. The casserole dishes could just as well be empty. What is in them is of no great importance; they are just a prop. The dishes are an excuse for the women to be where they know they should be. Being there is more important than anything else. God's presence is most likely to be known and felt in

3. Felton and Procter-Murphy, *Living the Questions*, 186.

the presence of caring persons who get there, who surround the one who is hurting. The clearest indication of God's presence is compassionate people.

In the way of a conclusion, I return to how I began. The attributes of God are images of human creation, expressed metaphorically, and open to more than one interpretation. God is omnipotent but does not control every detail of our existence. God is omniscient, but there are things he cannot know. God is immutable but moving with us. God is omnipresent, constant and unwavering. God is steadfast love, and this is the attribute that is specifically biblical and that we can participate in most fully.

One reason for the reappraisal of the attributes of God is to point out where they are misleading. By adopting a more open and flexible understanding of them it is possible to address a few problems. For one, the problem of how a loving and all-powerful God can allow bad things to happen to good people. The problem of theodicy is given a new dimension. A loving and all-powerful God would not be controlling every last little thing. For another, the pressure on each of us to discover the plan God has for us, and to follow that plan, is relieved. Having given us free will, God cannot know what we may choose to do in every situation. Without that knowledge a comprehensive plan for each of us is out of the question.

Another reason for the reappraisal of the attributes of God is that it serves to reinforce our belief in the immanence of God. We are not responsible for convincing God, by our good behavior, correct belief, or persistence in prayer, to intervene and miraculously make thing better. God is with us always and everywhere. From his side, we are never alone. From his side, our relationship with him is forever intact.

SIDEBAR

Process Theology

PROCESS THEOLOGY IS ONE alternative to the traditional theologies of the church. The process philosophy of Alfred North Whitehead provides the foundation for this theology.

According to process theology, a primary concern of God is the promotion of enjoyment throughout the creative process. Enjoyment is among God's fundamental aims.[1] To this end, God is the source of order. There can be little planning or progress without adequate order. Creative living and the enjoyment of life require a basic order and stability.[2]

God is also the source of disorder ("unrest" is the word used by John Cobb and David Ray Griffin). Unrest allows for the introduction of novelty, and it is novelty that provides enjoyment and zest. Excessive order is controlling, and for that reason detrimental to a full and enjoyable life.[3] Novelty produces freshness and interest, making life more full and rich. Novelty brings excitement to life, humor into a story, laughter at a joke. As a joke is told, one is led in a given direction, then, unexpectedly, a novel twist or turn is introduced, producing humor, bringing laughter. Life without novelty is drab. In *A Swiftly Tilting Planet*, Madeleine L'Engle writes of a joy

---

1. Cobb and Griffin, *Process Theology*, 56.
2. Cobb and Griffin, *Process Theology*, 59.
3. Cobb and Griffin, *Process Theology*, 61.

without which the universe would fall apart and collapse.[4] God, through introducing "unrest," and novelty, is the source of this joy.

The disorder and novelty introduced by God is adventuresome and risky. It is risky for God, and risky for us. As we assimilate and incorporate novelty we become engaged in the process of creation. And, as we are free agents, how we may respond to the opportunities and risks faced in novel situations that cannot be known beforehand. God cannot be in complete control of the outcome of the many twists and turns we take throughout life. Every detail of the process is not planned or ordered. Order is a derivative of novelty. Each novel event stabilizes, providing order, only to be destabilized by the next novel event in the process, which, in its turn provides stability and order again. This describes creation as moving forward, life looking ahead to what it may become, not looking back to what it may have been.

Under the hand of God, creation is in process, moving forward toward fullness and joy. Jesus is recorded as saying, "I have come that men may have life and have it in all its fullness" (John 10:10 NEB). We are being drawn by God into a relationship that is creative, dynamic, and in process. All of creation is being urged forward, wooed into a more full and enjoyable existence.

4. L'Engle, *Swiftly Tilting Planet*, 51.

12

Numbers and Relations

I DON'T BELIEVE THE doctrine of the Trinity is about numbers. Rather, I believe it portrays the inner life of God. It is an attempt to reconcile the divinity of Jesus with the divinity of God within the framework of monotheism. It is about the relationships of Father, Son, and Holy Spirit among themselves and with us.

The monotheism of Judaism was inherited by the early Christians, who were themselves Israelites. They believed that there was one God, and one God only. But this belief was disturbed by their experiences with Jesus. He was healing the sick, offering forgiveness, and teaching with self-affirmed authority. Jesus' life, death, and resurrection moved his followers to ascribe to him attributes traditionally reserved for God. Consequently, the image of God held by those early Christians was pulled in three directions. There was the God of their fathers, Abraham, Isaac, and Jacob. There was God's Spirit, his life-giving breath, active throughout the world. There was Jesus of Nazareth, now being given divine attributes. It is with this threefold experience that we begin.

Throughout the history and development of philosophy, there is a recurring theory that we know no thing in any absolute sense. We know only our experience of it. We do not know any thing, place, or person in itself. This is surely true of our knowledge of other persons, and particularly true of our knowledge of God. Rather than an illustration, I offer a truism. Any man who thinks he fully knows and understands his wife is delusional. To this may be added, any man who thinks he knows and understands God is dangerous. If we had a full knowledge of God, he would not be God, but something less even than we ourselves, whom we fail to understand. We do not know God. We know only our experience of God. The full mystery is beyond our comprehension. Consequently, we speak of God in metaphorical images.

In that the Bible is our primary record of humanity's experiences of God—Father, Son, and Spirit—it could be expected that the doctrine of the Trinity would be clearly articulated in the Bible. It is not; the word "Trinity" is not found in the Bible. There are intimations, but no specific declaration. The clearest intimations are found in the writings of St. Paul and in Matthew's Gospel. St. Paul wrote, "There are varieties of gifts, but the same Spirit. There are varieties of service, but the same Lord. There are many forms of work, but all of them, in all men, are the work of the same God" (1 Cor 12:4 NEB). St. Paul also wrote: "The grace of the Lord Jesus Christ, and the love of God, and fellowship in the Holy Spirit, be with you all" (2 Cor 13:14 NEB). At the conclusion of Matthew's Gospel there is a passage called "the Great Commission," in which Jesus instructs his disciples, "Go forth therefore and make all nations my disciples; baptize men everywhere in the name of the Father and the Son and the Holy Spirit, and teach them to observe all that I have commanded you" (Matt 28:19 NEB). These few passages are clearly trinitarian in nature but fall short of being any kind of explanation or doctrinal statement.

It is, perhaps, because of the lack of a definite statement in the Bible that trinitarian language was vague in the early development of Christianity. The first hint of a doctrine of the Trinity is not found until 180 CE, in the writings of Theophilus, bishop of Antioch. He used the Greek word for triad, *trias*, when referring to God.[1] It took many years for this early hint to become the doctrine of the Trinity that declares God to be three persons in one substance. It was much later, at the Council of Nicaea in 325 CE, and at the Council of Constantinople in 381, that a concept of a trinitarian God was used to defend the Christian faith against the heresies of the time. Arianism denied the divinity of Jesus, and too completely separated the persons of the Trinity, and Monarchianism too tightly unified them.

Ancient creeds, such as the Apostles' Creed (of early origin, but not composed by the apostles), and the Nicene Creed (that takes its name from the Council of Nicaea) are trinitarian in structure. They are organized into

---

1. Cross and Livingston, eds., *Oxford Dictionary of the Christian Church*, s.v. "Trinity."

three confessions: belief in God the Father, belief in God the Son, and belief in God the Holy Spirit. The Creed of St. Athanasius does not have the three-part structure of the other creeds but is strongly trinitarian. Though its authorship and date are in question, it may have been written as late as the sixth century. The many years between Theophilus in the second century and the Athanasian Creed in the sixth century illustrate the very slow development and acceptance of the doctrine of the Trinity. And the tedious explanation in the Athanasian Creed of every facet of the Trinity demonstrates that continuous reinterpretation went on for hundreds of years.

The need for reinterpretation continues into our time for the reason that our understanding of life and the world have changed drastically in the last few centuries. We now hold a scientific worldview that did not exist when the doctrine of the Trinity was developed, and the historic creeds written. And, in a world defined in scientific terms, substance becomes matter, and with three persons in one substance, a confusing definition of a God who is spirit. A better description of the Trinity may be found in the terms used by John Macquarrie. He describes God as one subsistence[2] (timeless, abstract existence), in three movements[3] experienced by we humans. What we have here is an image of God experienced in the dynamic movement within the life of God, throughout creation, and among us. This image is not to be taken literally, but as a description of our human experience of God.

To approach the Trinity as an image of the dynamic movements of God toward a relation with us brings us around to an entirely new perspective on ourselves. For this perspective, the place to begin is with the creation myth in the book of Genesis. Specifically, we turn to the statement that we are created in the image of God, "So, God created man in his own image; in the image of God he created him; male and female he created them" (Gen 1:27 NEB). When the primary image of God is the Trinity, then this is the image in which we are created. Every human person is created in the image of God described as one subsistence experienced in three persons, movements, faces. There is a mystery in this image of social, communal, reciprocal relatedness within one God. And there have been any number of attempts to find a symbol for this mystery. The shamrock is one; water, ice, and steam is another. The Father as lover, the Son as the beloved, and the Spirit as the love that flows between them, attributed to St. Augustine, is better for its sense of dynamic relations.

2. Macquarrie, *Principles of Christian Theology*, 299.
3. Macquarrie, *Principles of Christian Theology*, 193.

Part IV: God

The doctrine of the Trinity portrays the inner life of God as an engaging and animating love that does not allow for separation, or isolation, or solitude, or loneliness. In Trinity, God is dynamic and relational. The significance of this understanding of God is that it shows the nature of reality to be relational. We are created in the image of association, of community, of mutual loving care. We are created for life in relationships. It is not surprising that we are made ill by separation, isolation, and loneliness. We are created for each other.

Consequently, there is within us an innate awareness of the fundamental truth expressed in Jesus' Great Commandment, in the golden rule, and even in Immanuel Kant's categorical imperative. Jesus' Great Commandment may be summarized, "Love God with all that you are, and love others as you wish to be loved" (Mark 12:29–31). The idiomatic golden rule, "Do unto others as you would have them do unto you," expresses the second part of the Great Commandment. Kant's categorical imperative is somewhat more complex, but also more in keeping with our modern way of thinking: "Act only in accordance with that maxim through which you can at the same time will that it become a universal law."[4]

Our behavior should be conducive to healthy relations among persons and for the social networks in which we live. Life, certainly Christian life, is intended to be lived within a network of loving, supportive relationships. The relations within the life of God (Father, Son, and Spirit) is the model for our relations with one another.

My personality has led me to interpret the Trinity as being as much about us as it is about God. When I was serving a church in Overland Park, Kansas, a workshop was offered by the diocese to train the priests of the diocese in the use of the Myers-Briggs Personality Inventory. This inventory, among other things, is designed to evaluate a person's leanings toward introversion or extroversion. The workshop began one evening by having each of us take the inventory. The next day, the results were made known to each of us. Then came the question, "How many of you are extroverts?" About six or eight of us stood up. We were less than a fourth of the number of Episcopal priests in the room. All of the others were introverts. I was surprised by the division but gratified by what I learned about myself. For example, I have always repeated myself, saying things at least twice. I learned that, like many extroverts, my first response is "thinking out loud." The second response is much more likely to be what I really think and

4. Kant, *Groundwork for the Metaphysics of Morals*, 37.

114

mean. Before learning this, my excuse for talking so much was that as a pastor and preacher I made my living by the sweat of my tongue. I learned, also, that it is in consequence of my extroversion that I usually feel closer to God in a room full of noisy people than alone in a room during a silent retreat at which no one is supposed to speak.

For many years I took lessons to learn to play classical guitar, and I always took my guitar along for companionship in solitude. The following words are attributed to St. Augustine: "to sing once is to pray twice." I considered my playing music in some way to qualify as prayer. As a true extrovert, I am not good at being alone, and find that interacting with another person often puts me in mind of God. I write this so that other extroverts may take heart and find positive meaning in the doctrine of the Trinity.

Many people, not only extroverts, can find their relationship to God in their relationships with others: a loved one, or friend, a partner or mentor, or even just an acquaintance. And it is there, in our interactions with one another, that we work out our relationship with God. It is very difficult to be a Christian on our own. Our relation to others and to God are inseparable. Look again at the parable of the nations, in which Jesus said, "I tell you this: anything you did for one of my brothers here, however humble, you did for me" (Matt 25:40b NEB). This claim is then reinforced in the negative, "I tell you this, anything you did not do for one of these, however humble, you did not do for me" (Matt 25:45b NEB). It is said that Jesus never comes to anyone without bringing someone that person needs, or someone who needs that person. One Christian alone is no Christian, as pointed out by John Westerhoff III in several of his books. Christianity is a team sport, something that we do together. That we are not meant to be alone, and as Christians are never alone, is an important takeaway from the doctrine of the Trinity.

Trinity as symbol, image, or metaphor is a mystery. And, experiencing a mystery is one thing, explaining it is quite another. Trinity, as a figure of speech, is a description rather than an explanation. The doctrine of the Trinity is an attempt to put the complexity of our experience of God into words.

An intriguing imagining of God's unity is found in *The Ghost and Mrs. Muir*.[5] When speaking of the relationship between her daughter and son-in-law, Mrs. Muir affirms the strength of their union by saying, "they laugh in the same language." In our relationship with God, we should always

5. Dick, *Ghost and Mrs. Muir*, 163.

experience laughter. The distinct but inseparable faces of God (Father, Son, and Holy Spirit) are moments in one relationship of divine laughter and love. Trinity is a symbol of joyful relations. The moments of the Trinity are the "ways in which God is God."[6] Relating is God's way of being.

6. Norris, *Understanding the Faith of the Church*, 101.

SIDEBAR

Using the Trinity

THE TRINITY IS LIKE a flashlight. We don't look into the beam of a flashlight, or if we do, we have to blink and then for a few moments all we see are spots. The way to use a flashlight is to aim the beam at what we want to see more clearly and follow the beam. We all know that. But do we know how to use the Trinity as a flashlight? If we look directly into the Trinity, by taking it as a literal definition of God, we will only get spots in our mind's eye. We can, though, as if it were a beam of light, aim the Trinity on God and on ourselves. If we do it that way, we will see both more clearly.

When the beam of our trinitarian flashlight has been focused on God, as God the Father, a God of love has been seen. American Protestantism has taken John 3:16 as the centerpiece of its belief. "God loved the world so much that he gave his only Son, that everyone who has faith in him may not die but have eternal life" (John 3:16 NEB). There is a tongue-in-cheek version: "God so loved the world that he did not send a committee." The point being made by saying that God did not send a committee is that the world is not at the mercy of a system, but in the hands of a compassionate lover.

Love is a relationship, and in any relationship, there must be a comfortable degree of give and take. Even though each of us is a clumsy mix of good and bad, God accepts us. He gives and gives again. The beam of our flashlight will show that God the Father is engaged, in process with humanity, in an evolving relationship with us, possibly even getting dirty with us.

Focus the beam of our trinitarian flashlight on God the Son, on Jesus, and we get a good view of our dirty work. Dying on a cross is a very dirty business. Jesus did not set out to die. At some point in his life, he realized that he and the God he had come to call Father had become one. He went so far as to say, "My Father and I are one" (John 10:30 NEB). For the rest of his life, he was unflinchingly true to that realization. As few of us escape the consequences of our behavior, Jesus' death was the consequence of how he lived his life. A world that prizes power over compassion was sure to get him sooner or later, and repeatedly, as we turn away from him and deny his truth.

The beam of our flashlight shows that the disciples, and those other early followers of Jesus, soon realized that they were ascribing to Jesus attributes traditionally reserved for God. Jesus was creatively compassionate and accepting. Jesus had become the human face of God. In the beam of our trinitarian flashlight, in some incomprehensible way, the mystery of God can be seen in Jesus.

The mystery grows deeper when we train the beam of our trinitarian flashlight on God the Holy Spirit. Our culture's materialistic predisposition blinds us to the presence of the Spirit. And focusing our flashlight on the Spirit is made even more difficult because we will be looking at the reality of experience rather than at the reality of being. We will be looking at our experience of the presence of God rather than at God in himself. We cannot know God. If we could, he would not be God, but something less even than we are. What we can know is our experience of God, and that experience will be of the Spirit, an elusive and compassionate life force.

Now, as we turn the beam of our trinitarian flashlight on ourselves, we discover that the Trinity has a pronounced message for us. We, each and every one of us, is created in the image of God: "So, God created man in his own image; in the image of God he created him; male and female he created them" (Gen 1:27 NEB). That triune God (Father, Son, and Spirit) is a community. In God there is no aloneness, or loneliness, but compassionate relationships. And the relationships within God are the model for our relationships, for how we are to live with one another. Quite simply, the beam of our flashlight now shows that we are created for one another, to live in community and to support each other with compassionate care.

Obviously, there is no way to direct the beam of our trinitarian flashlight into every niche and corner. There is much that we will miss, or misunderstand, in the depth of the mystery of God and of life. Hopefully, we can begin to see that there is one God, one subsistence, experienced in three persons, three movements, three faces of compassion.

The Trinity can be used like a flashlight. It is not to be looked into as a definition of God, but to be looked with to light our way in the world. This flashlight is not a symbol of the Trinity, like the shamrock, or water as liquid, ice, and steam. It is a simile, like a suggestion as to how the Trinity may guide us into an ever more clear experience of God (Father, Son, and Spirit).

PART V

Spirit

13

Presence and Results

I DON'T BELIEVE WE experience the Spirit in a direct, overt way. Instead, we experience the results of the Spirit's presence. The Spirit is nebulous, intangible, and self-effacing. The Spirit is the face of God we never see, and for that reason we have no mental picture other than the symbols of dove, fire, and wind. These symbols will be addressed more fully in the next chapter. My purpose here is to explain that we know the Spirit only by the consequences of her presence, and to emphasize the presence of the Spirit as dynamic and powerful.

I have chosen to use the feminine personal pronoun for several reasons. In Hebrew, the word *ruach* can mean wind, breath, or spirit, and it is a feminine noun. In Greek, the word *pneuma* also means wind, breath, or spirit, and is neuter. The decision as to which of these three—wind, breath, spirit—is the correct interpretation depends upon the context. And the decision to write of the Spirit as feminine is determined by the belief that, though God is beyond categories of gender, using the feminine personal pronoun portrays God as more complete and inclusive.

Feminine as well as masculine images for God are used throughout the Bible. There are clear examples of feminine images in the prophets. Speaking for God, Isaiah wrote, "Long have I lain still, I kept silence and held myself in check; now I will cry like a woman in labor, whimpering, panting and gasping" (Isa 42:14 NEB). Hosea wrote, "I will meet them like a she-bear robbed of her cubs and tear their ribs apart, like a lioness I will devour them on the spot" (Hos 13:8 NEB). These two passages, and there are many more, do not prove that God is feminine, just as the male images do not prove that God is masculine.

Continuing with the prophets of the Old Testament, the presence and activity of the Spirit in inspiring these men is found in the results. Even when one is inspired, there may be nothing to see. One must trust the inspiration, which may come as a feeling, an inclination, an urge, a passion, or just an "itch." In consequence of the Spirit's persuasion, the prophet speaks. We begin with the prophet Amos, a shepherd and farmer in Tekoa, a small town in Judah about ten miles from Jerusalem. He lived in the middle of the eighth century BCE. Amos was inspired to speak as the consequence of a number of visions that revealed to him the sins of Israel. We read what the Lord "showed" him, which led him to write, "Let justice roll on like a river and righteousness like an ever-flowing stream" (Amos 5:24 NEB). We read much the same message in the prophet Micah: "God has told you what is good; and what it is that the Lord asks of you? Only to act justly, to love loyalty, to walk wisely before your God" (Mic 6:8 NEB). The prophet Isaiah, whose writings underwent a final editing around the beginning of the fourth century BCE, also made a clear demand for justice. There is a consistency in the message for hundreds of years as the Spirit inspired prophet after prophet to speak for God. And, always, we get the message through the voice of a spokesman, as the Spirit remains behind the scenes.

In the prophet Isaiah, the opening verses of chapter 61 are important for continuing the message found in Amos and Micah, and also as a bridge between the prophets and Jesus. Jesus chose to read these verses as part of what is called his inaugural address, found in the Gospel according to Luke. The wording of the two passages, from Isaiah and Luke, are almost the same, and I have chosen to quote the version found in Luke. "The spirit of the Lord is upon me because he has anointed me; he has sent me to announce good news to the poor, to proclaim release for prisoners and recovery of sight for the blind; to let the broken victims go free, to proclaim the year of the Lord's favour" (Luke 4:18–19 NEB). Jesus, under the influence of the Spirit, is proclaiming the end of Israel's exile, God's return to Zion, and the coming of God's kingdom. In his call for justice and concern for the dispossessed, there is a consistency of message from the prophets to Jesus, all under the influence of the Spirit. Although the inspiration is palpable and the message clear, the Spirit never exposes herself.

The Spirit was producer and director at the birth of Jesus, but still from behind the scenes. An angel told Mary, "The Holy Spirit will come upon you and the power of the Most High will over shadow you; and for that reason the holy child to be born will be called 'Son of God'" (Luke 1:35 NEB). This same Spirit revealed herself at the baptism of Jesus. "At the moment when he came up out of the water, he saw the heavens torn open and the Spirit, like a dove descending upon him" (Mark 1:10 NEB). The pattern is much the same in the recognition of Jesus. "'What about you?' he asked them. 'Who do you say I am?' Simon Peter answered, 'You are the Messiah, the Son of the living God.' 'Good for you, Simon son of John!' answered Jesus. 'For this truth did not come to you from any human being, but it was given to you directly by my Father in heaven'" (Matt 16:15–17 GN). In all three of these stories, one from each of the first three Gospels, we have the Spirit's actions and influence, but from behind the scenes.

From these three scenes, it is apparent that the actions of the Spirit depend upon a human response for those actions to come to fruition. Mary was humble and accepting, Jesus was open and responsive, Peter was bold and ready. The biblical record shows synergistic cooperation between the Spirit and a human person that eventually brings results.

My own experience with the Spirit, as I have come to understand that experience, happened when I was confronted by a friend. The Very Rev. Urban T. Holmes III, onetime dean of the school of theology at the University of the South, was the Episcopal chaplain at LSU when I was a student. In my last semester at LSU I joined the National Guard and was attached to the Army for six months active duty for training. My period of training was divided between Fort Chaffee, Arkansas, and Fort Sam Houston, San Antonio, Texas. While in San Antonio, I found an Episcopal church that was a short distance outside one of the gates and began attending church again. Eventually, I began to consider the possibility of entering the ministry. Back in Baton Rouge, when I had completed my six months for training, I began to hang around the Episcopal Student Center at LSU. I was interested in a series of lectures on church history, and in a pretty co-ed who was willing to go out with me. Subconsciously, no doubt, there was another reason for my frequenting the student center, and Chaplain Holmes sensed it. I cannot remember the exact day or time when he confronted me, but I do have a clear memory of the circumstances. I was in a sort of enclosed walkway across the front of the student center that connected the chapel and fellowship hall. Chaplain Holmes stepped in front of me. Even though I am six feet, one inch tall and weigh two hundred pounds, he dwarfed me. He was a very big man, and a man I respected. He said to me, in no uncertain terms, "Why don't you stop putting it off, and make up your mind to go to seminary?" In an instant, I did just that. The following August, 1959, I entered the school of theology of the University of the South. I have never forgotten those few minutes when Chaplain Holmes stopped me in my tracks. I have never regretted the decision I made that day. The Spirit was not discernible to me in any manner I could conceptualize, but when she speaks through a very big man, she is strongly persuasive. She can, as well, act through any mediator of any description.

Just as in my own experience, various events reported in the New Testament attest to the persuasiveness of the Spirit. The Spirit can empower: "Then Jesus, armed with the power of the Spirit, returned to Galilee; and reports about him spread through the whole country-side" (Luke 4:14 NEB). The Spirit can bring truth: "However, when he comes who is the spirit of truth, he will guide you into all truth" (John 16:13a NEB). The Spirit is liberating: "And where the Spirit of the Lord is, there is liberty" (2 Cor 3:17b NEB). These verses are pulled out of context, but even so, they show again that we get the Spirit's gifts, but never the Spirit herself clearly before our eyes. Consequently, we often attribute our experience to some cause that has nothing to do with the Spirit or with God.

There is one additional area in which the influence of the Spirit can be considered, and that is new life. Jesus was approached by a Pharisee named Nicodemus, a member of the Jewish Council, who came to him at night. "'Rabbi,' he said, 'we know that you are a teacher sent by God; no one could perform these signs of yours unless God were with him.'" Jesus' response to this ingratiating approach only confused Nicodemus, leading Jesus to continue, "In truth I tell you, no one can enter the kingdom of God without being born from water and spirit" (John 3:5 NEB). Jesus spoke of the water of cleansing, not necessarily of baptism, and the power of the Spirit for reconciliation and new life. When the Spirit cooperates in the saving work of Jesus, there is no division, no separation between the work of Christ and of the Spirit.

Holmes has an interesting explanation of the dynamics of salvation. He points out that the Greek verb translated into English as "to save" is *soso*. In turn, that Greek word is a translation of the Hebrew word *yashah*. *Yashah* means "to make spacious," or "to make roomy." Here it is necessary to make the point that the word "repentance" in biblical usage does not mean to be sorry—that is "penitence." To repent is to turn, or return, to God. In the New Testament, repentance is a full reorientation of life, a full turn to a better direction in life. The life of Mary Magdalene is the illustration Holmes uses in his explanation of salvation as making room. Assumed to be a prostitute, Mary was labeled as such and hemmed in by the attitudes of those around her. Society allowed her no space in which to move, no room in which to turn her life around and find a new and better direction. Jesus saved her by giving her the space she needed to turn her life around.[1] He called her no names. He reconciled her to God, to himself, and to others by giving her the room to find a new life and become a better person. He did not press her back into the role of a prostitute, nor did he press her to move ahead. Rather, he accepted her for who she was, and in doing so he lifted her out of the sordid restrictions of her former life, freeing her to become healed, whole, and safe.

To this day the Spirit continues the work of Jesus. Just as Jesus did not press, she does not press, but inspires, enlightens, persuades. The Spirit does not force or manipulate, but works within, an internal influence. The operation of the Spirit I offer is supported by St. Paul. "But you are not in the flesh; you are in the Spirit, since the Spirit of God dwells in you" (Rom 8:9 NRSV). This work in us, from within, does not make the Spirit any less moving or dramatic. It does, though, leave us without any perceivable image. We have no picture of the Spirit in our mind's eye. Other than a dove, wind, and fire, we have no physical image, and these three are only symbols expressed in metaphor and simile.

As I have been pointing out, even without any direct evidence of the Spirit's presence, we do have the consequences of the Spirit's presence, the results of her inspiring influence. These results can, of course, be attributed to any number of other possible influences and causes. There is, though, one way of living in which the presence of the Spirit is unmistaken, when there is an uptick in doing justice, caring for the downtrodden, and faithfulness in relationships. From one side, there is a correlation between behavior and the teachings of the prophets, particularly as regards those passages discussed above. From the other side, there is an adherence to the work and words of Jesus, "Be compassionate as your Father is compassionate" (Luke 6:36 NEB). When we are moved to selfish concern for ourselves, we are listening only to the voice of our own inclinations, but when we are

---

1. Holmes, *Turning to Christ*, 158–59.

moved toward others, with empathy, compassion, and love, we are, by the grace of God, responding to the voice of the Spirit within us.

The grace of God is an expression of God's compassion. In the Old Testament, grace is God's good favor, his gift of enjoyment, his offer of a relationship with himself. In the New Testament God's grace is expressed clearly. "But God, rich in mercy [compassion], for the great love he bore for us, brought us to life with Christ even when we were dead in our sins; it is by his grace you are saved" (Eph 2:4–5 NEB). The grace of God is his freely given, unmerited favor and love.

As expressed in an earlier chapter, grace is God's gift to us of himself. The Spirit is the pervader of that gift. The work of grace within human persons is the province of the Spirit. She is the dynamic energy of God on our behalf. The Spirit is truly God, fully God, a face of God we never see. The Spirit is herself the gift of grace.

SIDEBAR

Frontier Theology

TWO DECIDEDLY AMERICAN IMAGES of the Holy Spirit are offered in the book *Western Theology*, written and illustrated by Wes Seeliger. He makes a distinction in our images of the Spirit by designating one "settler theology," and the other "pioneer theology."

In settler theology, the image is feminine. The Spirit is Miss Dove, who runs the Olive Branch Saloon. She is charming, and her saloon is warm and cozy. It is located right next to the sheriff's office. Anyone old enough to have watched the TV series *Gunsmoke* will remember Miss Kitty, the saloonkeeper played by Amanda Blake. The show starred James Arness as Marshall Dillon, and ran for twenty seasons. Like Miss Kitty, Miss Dove fits right into American folklore. Miss Dove's bartender, Norman Spill, completes the image of the Spirit. Norman is a good listener and has a good word for everyone. He gives advice and tells folks to think positively. Miss Dove and Norman offer comfort to the settlers and help them face their troubles.[1]

In pioneer theology, the Spirit is Wild Red, a huge and awesome buffalo hunter with red hair. It is his job to furnish fresh meat, without which the pioneers would starve. Wild Red is a prankster with a weird sense of humor who rides a half-tame buffalo named Pentecost. Wild Red is too unpredictable for the settlers, who find him downright frightening.

---

1. Seeliger, *Western Theology*, 47–49.

While the settler's concern is for safety, the pioneer's concern is for following the Spirit in a world that is forever changing, unpredictable, and sometimes dangerous.[2] The author of Hebrews encourages us to look to Jesus " the pioneer and perfecter of our faith" (Heb 12:2 NRSV). We need a robust image of the Spirit, a Wild Red, if we are to persevere and take life in stride.

The need for Miss Dove is not to be denied, but there may be a greater need for Wild Red. Churches can sometimes become too settled to respond well to the exploits of Wild Red, but a settled, complacent church can become a boring church, and a boring church is a dying church.

---

2. Seeliger, *Western Theology,* 51–53.

14

Safe or Close

I DON'T BELIEVE THE purpose of the Spirit is to keep us safe. Though always close, the Spirit will not protect us from the risks inherent in our freedom. The Spirit's closeness will be considered from three perspectives: first, on a continuum from providence, to chance, to luck; second, in light of the biblical images of dove, fire, and wind; and third, according to the significance of considering the Spirit our paraclete.

The first perspective follows the continuum that begins with the providence of God. His providence, his protective care, operates very differently from what we are taught to expect. A proper understanding of the attributes of God, discussed in chapter 11, shows that God is not guiding, much less controlling or manipulating every earthly occurrence and outcome. God does not have a specific plan for anyone's life; we are free to set our own goals. He does not lift us out of, or above, the natural flow of life, nor does he protect us from the consequences of our behavior. God joins us in this life, and that is the story of Jesus. He accompanies us, and that is the province of the Spirit.

To get to the province of the Spirit, we move from providence to chance. God took a chance on Jesus, who was a real person with the freedom to say to God, "No!" Jesus took a chance on God and what he thought God expected of him. I am relying here, and in the next two paragraphs, on the arguments of Robert Farrar Capon. Jesus was not kept safe from the ordeal of crucifixion; he died on a cross. He was not lifted out of, or above, the consequences of how he lived his life in this world. In this world, he died. The world was saved on the cross, not saved from it.[1] God chose then, and he chooses now, not to intervene. It was not until after the death of Jesus that God made his move to show us that, though chance involves risk, we are in the hands of a lover rather than in the grip of a system of just deserts.

We turn to God for help in navigating the risky business of life, but the only promise we have from God is that he will be with us, no matter what. To God, good luck or bad luck are much the same. Each is just as good as the other for the ground of his relationship with us. An expression of this is found in Matthew's Gospel: "But what I tell you is this: love your enemies and pray for your persecutors; only so can you be children of your heavenly Father, who makes his sun rise on good and bad alike, and sends rain on the honest and the dishonest" (Matt 5:44–45 NEB). This passage can be interpreted as an expression of God's preference for a level playing field. He is not trying to fix things, or in any way "jimmy" the outcome. His Spirit is not out to save us from what life may throw at us. As a mode of operation, luck seems to serve God's purpose better than meddling.

Capon admits that we are uncomfortable with this God of luck. From our point of view, he is not a respectable God. A God who favors luck, who fails to award the good and punish the bad, appears to be unfair. No respectable judge would operate in such a manner. But all our efforts to turn a risky love into a safe system have come to no effect, or have made matters worse. By drawing up rules and regulations that only keep people out of a relationship God wants them to be in, the church becomes less like Christ. Only love will prevent us from doing all the wrong things in our effort to make things come out right. Operating by luck does not rule out love, for the reason that luck does not determine the outcome, but is only our evaluation of the outcome. When something befalls us, we call it good or bad according to how it affects us. Luck is neutral—it has no stake in the outcome.

We who live along the coastline of the Gulf of Mexico, from the tip of Florida to the bottom of Texas, understand risk and the chance of being in harm's way. My wife, Margene, and I were newlyweds in New Orleans, in 1965, when Hurricane Betsy ripped through the city. We were living in Slidell, on the north shore of Lake Pontchatrain, in 1969, when Hurricane Camille blew through the area. And, in 2005, when Hurricane Katrina slammed into the Mississippi Gulf Coast, we were living in Waveland, which happened to be ground zero. The cottage in which we were living,

1. Capon, *Health, Money, and Love*, 167.

a cottage we had purchased in 1967 as our retirement home, was totally destroyed. So, too, was every house destroyed, in every direction from ours, as far as the eye could see. Except for the family albums and memorabilia we took with us when we evacuated, all was lost, including the library I had been developing since my days in college. The death of one of my brothers was the greatest loss. He made the fatal decision to stay in my sister's house across the street from mine in Waveland. The force of a hurricane can do terrible damage, and when the wind is pushing a wall of water over twenty-five feet high the destruction is cataclysmic.

That, however, is not the whole story. For a considerable length of time after the storm, because of the damage done to cell towers, we had no telephone communication. Our phones were useless, so we reverted to the use of notes and notices that could be posted in Gallery 220 at the corner of Main and Toulme Streets in downtown Bay Saint Louis. On one occasion, when checking the notices, I saw that a friend was issuing an open invitation to a "bring-your-own-meat" cookout on his property. I say "property" because his home was gone. Evidently, a couple of grills had been salvaged from the debris left behind by the storm. Around fifty people showed up, and not one person there had a home left standing. Most of the people knew each other but had not seen each other since before Hurricane Katrina made landfall. People were running up to one another, happy at finding their friends, full of questions and anecdotes, needing to exchange survival stories. There was an underlying hum of feeling, a sense of having undergone together a very difficult and wrenching time. We had been torn apart by wind and water, and then blown back together again by the Spirit. We were not kept safe by the Spirit, but we were kept together. That cookout became an unforgettable experience.

The second perspective to take into consideration is found in the three primary symbols of the Spirit in the New Testament (dove, fire, and wind). The dove appears at the baptism of Jesus, an event recorded in all four Gospels. And, though we have four accounts, there was only a single appearance of "the Spirit, like a dove." The original account is in Mark's Gospel. "At the moment when he [Jesus] came up out of the water, he saw the heavens torn open and the Spirit, like a dove, descending upon him" (Mark 1:10 NEB). The dove was a sacred bird in Palestine, according to William Barclay.[2] Consequently the dove was an obvious and ready symbol to choose for the Spirit. It is important to note that in all four Gospels (Mark 1:10;

2. Barclay, *Gospel of John*, 83.

Matthew 3:16; Luke 3:22; John 1:32) the symbol of the dove is expressed as simile. The Spirit was "like a dove," and nowhere in the New Testament does it say that the Spirit is a dove. The dove is a beautiful symbol, easy to represent in art, but a bird is a weak representation of the powerful and dynamic presence of God.

Fire is a strong symbol, and it is a good symbol for the Spirit because fire can get out of hand. It is not always easy to control fire, and it is impossible to control the Spirit. Also, fire is a more complex symbol than a bird. We speak of someone burning with passion for an idea, or project, or cause. The primary source of this symbol is found in the Acts of the Apostles. "While the Day of Pentecost was running its course they were all together in one place, when suddenly there came from the sky a noise like that of a strong driving wind, which filled the whole house where they were sitting. And there appeared to them tongues like flames of fire dispersed among them and resting on each one. And they were filled with the Holy Spirit (Acts 2:1–4a NEB). In this instance, as in the case of the dove, fire is not a direct image of the Spirit, but a symbol expressed as simile, as "tongues like flames of fire" appeared to them. This is a potent symbol of the Spirit but does not represent well the Spirit as the personal presence of God. Fire has no compassion.

Wind is a more dramatic symbol of the Spirit, because, as pointed out in the previous chapter, in both major biblical languages, the word for wind can also mean breath or spirit. In the opening pages of the Bible, breath is associated with God-given life. The second creation story tells of God breathing life into man: "The Lord God formed a man from the dust of the ground and breathed into his nostrils the breath of life" (Gen 2:7 NEB). And our common experience is that without breath there is no life. God as the source of breath and life is also found in the New Testament. St. Paul, in his address to the men of Athens in the court of Areopagus, said, "It is not because he [God] lacks anything that he accepts service at men's hands, for he is himself the universal giver of life and breath and all else" (Acts 17:25 NEB). The description of the coming of the Spirit on the day of Pentecost, as fire and as wind, is vibrant and intense. The symbol of the Spirit as driving wind is found also in the Gospel according to John. Because he is a literalist, Nicodemus is unable to understand what Jesus is saying about being born from above. Jesus is astonished that Nicodemus is unable to understand, and he attempts to explain, "The wind blows where it will; you hear the sound of it, but you do not know where it comes from, or where it is going. So with everyone who is born from spirit" (John 3:8 NEB). Jesus is using a complex metaphor, and by its very complexity it provides a good picture of the Spirit as mysteriously unknown, and beyond our control. The complexity lies in the word *pneuma* being translated sometimes as wind and sometimes as spirit throughout the passage just quoted.

The richness of these symbols, dove, wind, and fire, is shown in Christian art, in church design, and in how they show up in literature.

A third perspective of the Spirit is found in the Greek word *parakletos*, which is used in reference to the Spirit in John's Gospel. This word is used for the Spirit only in John, but it appears there in four different passages: 14:16, 14:26; 15:26; and 16:7. This is a difficult word to translate into English. The first half of it, though, *para*, which means "with," has found its way into our language as a prefix: "paramedic," "paralegal," "paranormal," for a few examples. The second half of the word means "to call." The English version of the word is "paraclete," one who is called to accompany us, called to be with us.

In the earlier English translations of the Bible, the paraclete was the "Helper." This is a reasonably good translation and is still used in the Good News Bible. "But I am telling you the truth: it is better for you that I go away, because if I do not go, the Helper will not come to you" (John 16:7 GN). This passage implies that the Spirit is the closeness of God, here to help. In the King James Version of the Bible, the paraclete is the "Comforter." "But when the Comforter is come, whom I will send unto you from the Father, even the Spirit of truth, which proceedeth from the Father, he shall testify of me" (John 15:26 KJV).

In the seventeenth century, Comforter was a good enough translation. At the time, to comfort was to strengthen. The second part of the word, "fort," is from the Latin word *fortis*, meaning strong, and from which we get the word "fortress." Today, however, "comforter" is a softer word, meaning to console. Comfort now amounts to holding someone's hand and saying everything will be all right, even at times when we know it will not. The Spirit does, of course, offer comfort, but comfort now proposes too small a role for the Spirit. In the New English Bible and the New Revised Standard Version, the paraclete is an "Advocate," with the NRSV giving "Helper" as an alternative by means of a footnote. "But the Advocate, the Holy Spirit, whom the Father will send in my name, will teach you everything and remind you of all that I have said to you" (John 14:26 NRSV). The shortcoming of *Advocate* is its forensic connotation, denoting one who is called into court to witness for the defense. A broader meaning is needed, for the Spirit is not only a witness in our defense, but also a witness to the presence of God.

Actually, the first use of paraclete in the Gospel according to John, by including the phrase "who will be with you," provides a more accurate understanding of the word. "I will ask the Father, and he will give you another to be your Advocate, who will be with you for ever—the Spirit of truth" (John 14:16 NEB). The Spirit is God with us forever.

A full and adequate picture of the Spirit as our paraclete is provided by bringing together all the possible meanings of the word. No one of these various meanings indicate that the Spirit will, in any miraculous way, keep us safe, protected from the normal ups and downs of life in this world. Even so, by keeping close, the Spirit is our helper in difficult times. The Spirit gives us strength to be brave when we are in fear. The Spirit is a witness on our behalf when we wander. Above all, the Spirit is God walking with us, side by side.

God's presence, compassion, and love are not determined by a run of good luck, or of bad. His Spirit, without ever being meddlesome, is forever present, our companion. The biblical symbols (dove, fire, and wind), though not always adequate, give us ways to conceptualize the Spirit, and to portray her in art and literature. And, though we know the Spirit only indirectly, through the voice of another, she is close by, walking with us, God most immanent.

SIDEBAR

Blaspheming the Spirit

JESUS MADE A COMMENT on the Spirit and forgiveness that deserves consideration. It is, "Truly I tell you, people will be forgiven their sins and whatever blasphemies they utter; but whoever blasphemes against the Holy spirit can never have forgiveness" (Mark 3:28–29 NRSV). This statement can also be found in Matthew (12:31) and Luke (12:10).

Biblical commentators interpret this passage to mean that when a person is so twisted that they perceive good as evil and evil as good there is no hope for that person. If one thinks the Spirit of God evil enough to curse, there is then no way for the Spirit to have any positive effect. When the good that approaches is considered evil and resisted while what is evil is not resisted, no remedy has a chance.

Conspiracy theories cross the line between what is acceptable and what is unacceptable in a society that claims to be good, moral, and Christian. Those who concoct or spread conspiracy theories approach that line beyond which good and evil are reversed. Specifically, to accuse the parents whose children where slain in a school shooting of being actors staging a fake tragedy is despicable. To twist the truth in such a way as to cause those parents greater grief is akin to reversing good and evil. When a person creates or spreads an unfounded theory that is designed to make good look evil, that person has moved into what the Gospels call blaspheming the Holy Spirit.

Part V: Spirit

Blaspheming the Holy Spirit stems from a reversal of morals and ethics. This is to have good and evil backwards. It is to become so twisted and turned about that response to the Spirit of God becomes impossible, and forgiveness cannot be received.

15

Spirituality and Goodness

I DON'T BELIEVE SPIRITUALITY is about God and me. Many years ago, a friend of mine wrote: "Jesus didn't die on the cross to create a lot of little 'Me and God' clubs." At its best, Christian spirituality is about us, and about us at our best. We are at our best when we seek an open relationship with God in which others have important places. There can be no private spirituality.

The spirituality of Celtic Christianity speaks to and strengthens the communal side of traditional Christian spirituality. Celtic spirituality contributes its core belief in the essential goodness of creation, and its belief that the image of God present in all persons can never be totally obscured. A private spirituality might be defended in a world so degraded by evil that all the world had gone completely wrong. Celtic Spirituality, however, embraces creation as good because God is at the heart of his world.[1]

Before continuing with Celtic Christianity, the influence of St. Augustine of Hippo and of John Calvin must be considered. St. Augustine, one of the most influential theologians in Western Christianity, was a brilliant neurotic. Born in 354 CE in North Africa, he did not become a Christian until 386, after living a rather wild life as a young man. In response to pagan claims that the fall of Rome in 410 was due to the worship of God rather than pagan deities, St. Augustine affirmed the essential goodness of

1. Newell, *Listening to the Heartbeat of God*, 3–4.

creation and defined evil as the absence of good.[2] Even so, he had a very low opinion of mankind. He believed the disobedience of Adam and Eve, and their fall from grace, infected mankind with a congenital moral disease.[3] Because of his literal interpretation of the creation myth in the book of Genesis, he came to believe that due to the fallen nature of mankind, we are at odds with ourselves and dead in spirit.[4] If St. Augustine did not actually "invent" the doctrine of original sin, he certainly made it a central doctrine in Western Christianity. For further information on original sin, turn to the Sidebar to chapter 3.

John Calvin, a French reformer and theologian who lived from 1509 to 1564, condemned human nature even more severely than did St. Augustine. A rigid authoritarian, Calvin taught that man's fall from grace brought about so critical a degradation of human nature that everything humans will or do is sinful. The pervasiveness of the fall alienated all of creation from God.[5]

Celtic spirituality provides a positive alternative to the more pessimistic theologies of St. Augustine and of Calvin. Take, for example, the teachings of Pelagius, a Celtic Briton who engaged St. Augustine in a serious controversy. Pelagius, the eponymous founder of Pelagianism, held that human persons can take the initiative, and by their own efforts achieve their salvation. St. Augustine, with his belief in original sin, won the debate, and Pelagius was declared a heretic. Pelagius, however, was not all wrong. He was correct in stressing the essential goodness of creation and the image of God in all persons.[6] A potential Celtic contribution to Christianity was lost.

Celtic spirituality recognizes the darkness caused by our selfish disregard for one another. Even so, it celebrates the streaks of light brought into every life by the presence of the Spirit. Through the presence of the Spirit, there are no gaps between earth and heaven, and even "thin places" where the material world is particularly close to the spiritual world.[7] Some locations have long been recognized as "thin places," Iona, for example, a small island off the west coast of Scotland. In 563 CE, St. Columba established a

2. Augustine, *City of God*, 440.

3. Augustine, *City of God*, 512.

4. Augustine, *City of God*, 575.

5. Cross and Livingston, eds., *Oxford Dictionary of the Christian Church*, s.v. "Calvinism."

6. Newell, *Listening to the Heartbeat of God*, 10.

7. Newell, *Listening to the Heartbeat of God*, 89.

monastery on Iona, and it became the cradle of Scottish Christianity. To this day it is considered a sacred place. It is possible, though, for any place to be a "thin place" when we become aware of the presence of the Spirit.

There are such "thin places" mentioned in the Old Testament. For example, Jacob experienced one while on his way from Beersheba to Harran. "At sunset he came to a holy place and camped there. He lay down to sleep, resting his head on a stone. He dreamed that he saw a stairway reaching from earth to heaven, with angels going up and coming down on it. And there was the Lord standing beside him. . . . Jacob woke up and said, 'The Lord is here! He is in this place, and I didn't know it!' He was afraid and said, 'What a terrifying place this is! It must be the house of God; it must be the gate that opens into heaven'" (Gen 28:10–17 GN). Jacob found himself in a "thin place," in the presence of the Lord. Moses provides a second example in the Old Testament.

> One day while Moses was taking care of the sheep and goats of his father-in-law Jethro, the priest of Midian, he led the flock across the desert and came to Sinai, the holy mountain. There the angel of the Lord appeared to him as a flame coming from the middle of a bush. Moses saw that the bush was on fire but that it was not burning up. "This is strange," he thought. "Why isn't the bush burning up? I will go closer and see." When the Lord saw that Moses was coming closer he called to him from the middle of the bush and said, "Moses! Moses!" He answered, "Yes, here I am." God said, "Do not come any closer. Take off your sandals, because you are standing on holy ground." (Exod 3:1–5 GN)

Moses realized that something out of the ordinary was happening, and when he went closer to look, he found himself in a "thin place."

For Jesus, because the Spirit was always with him, all of earth was a "thin place." That is a possible reading of the witness of John the Baptist: "And John gave this testimony: 'I saw the Spirit come down like a dove from heaven and stay on him. I still did not know that he was the one, but God, who sent me to baptize with water, had said to me, 'You will see the Spirit come down and stay on a man; he is the one who baptizes with the Holy Spirit'" (John 1:32–33 GN). The Spirit seen as staying on, or staying with Jesus, may be read as an expression of Jesus living in constant awareness of the Spirit, and of being always in a "thin place."

The rest of us experience the Spirit briefly and intermittently. I write this chapter on April 13, 2020, the Monday after Easter Sunday, in the middle of the COVID-19 pandemic. My wife and I, with our neighbors, are nearing the end of our first month of "sheltering in place" and social distancing, and anticipate additional months of the same. Yesterday, Easter Sunday, six of us, three couples who are immediate neighbors and good friends, got together, almost, under the carport of one. "Almost," I say, because we were careful to maintain the recommended six-foot distance from couple to couple. I celebrated Holy Communion, in its briefest form, at 11:30 in the morning, each couple having its own bread and wine. I believe God's blessings can reach across six feet of space. After the service, we had our mid-day Easter dinner, each couple eating its own meal, individually prepared. We then sat and visited, and drank wine, until almost four in the afternoon. For a few hours, we had Easter, we had each other, and we had a break from our anxieties. For a time, my neighbor's carport became a "thin place."

I continue now with what we can learn from Celtic spirituality. John Scotus Eriugena, a ninth-century philosopher from the Celtic branch of the church, taught that Christ moves among us in two shoes: Scripture and creation. Reading the Easter Gospel while sheltering against the threat of disease, the Bible and the virus, moved Christ among us in two shoes. Eriugena's belief that God is in all things, always and everywhere, was condemned by the church as pantheism, though, more accurately, it is panentheism. Another potential Celtic contribution to Christianity was lost. A philosophical expression of Eriugena's teaching is that goodness is not an attribute of being, but that being is an attribute of the goodness of God.[8]

Christian spirituality today is being enriched by the rediscovery of Celtic spirituality. The acknowledgement of God's presence throughout creation, and not only in those aspects that might be considered religious, guides us to celebrate the essential goodness of our world and of humanity. The Spirit is experienced as the unifying love in our relationship with God and in all our relationships. The world is interlaced with the presence of God, and every person is created in his indelible image. Celtic spirituality would not have us pull away from the world or from one another.

8. Newell, *Listening to the Heartbeat of God*, 36.

SIDEBAR

St. Patrick

ANY PRESENTATION OF CELTIC Christianity and Celtic spirituality would be incomplete if it did not include St. Patrick. To position his life historically within Celtic Christianity, it is necessary to look at what was happening to Roman Christianity. Between 406 and 419, much of the Roman Empire was lost to various Germanic tribes. The city of Rome was sacked by the Visigoths in 410, and the Western Empire came to an end in 476.[1] These defeats and the disruption they caused weakened the influence of the church in Rome. Consequently, the church in Britain was left to its own devices, allowing Celtic Christianity to spread and grow stronger.

St. Patrick was born into a Christian family around the year 390. When he was sixteen or so years old, he was captured by Irish slave-traders and taken to Ireland. There he was forced to serve as a shepherd. After six years, when he was about twenty-two years old, he escaped and returned to Britain, where he was educated as a Christian and eventually took holy orders. The Christianity to which he would have been exposed at that time in Britain was surely Celtic in expression. St. Patrick returned to Ireland as a bishop around 432. He was exceptionally successful as a missionary, establishing his principal church in Armagh. St. Patrick died around the year 460.[2]

1. MacCulloch, *Christianity*, 234.
2. Cross and Livingston, eds., *Oxford Dictionary of the Christian Church*, s.v. "Patrick."

His death occurred more than a century before the Roman mission to Britain, which did not take place until Pope Gregory the Great sent Augustine (not Augustine of Hippo) to convert the Anglo-Saxons to Christianity. Augustine, eventually known as Augustine of Canterbury, with a group of monks, landed in Kent in 597. To their great surprise, they discovered that Christianity already existed in Britain.[3] This would have been Celtic Christianity. Considering when he lived, St. Patrick's Celtic background cannot be denied.

St. Patrick wrote very little, and the hymn "St. Patrick's Breastplate" was probably not written by him. Even so, it is a sound expression of the Celtic Christianity of his time. The sixth verse, quoted here, clearly represents the beliefs of Celtic Christianity.

> Christ be with me, Christ within me,
> Christ behind me, Christ before me,
> Christ beside me, Christ to win me,
> Christ to comfort and restore me,
>
> Christ beneath me, Christ above me,
> Christ in quiet, Christ in danger,
> Christ in hearts of all that love me,
> Christ in mouth of friend and stranger.[4]

In Celtic spirituality, we are engulfed by the Christ of God, as is well expressed in this ancient hymn of the church.

3. MacCulloch, *Christianity*, 338.
4. Episcopal Church, *Hymnal 1982*, no. 370.

PART VI

Now

16

Flat or Round

I DON'T BELIEVE SUNDAY morning in church is relevant to the other days of the week. The church is using flat words in a round world. Those who put the church's teachings into words lived in a very small world. People of that day thought they lived on a flat world, at the center of creation, with the waters below and the heavens above. We know, today, that the world is round, circulating a small star in one galaxy among unnumbered galaxies. From that early time to now, our cosmology has matured, and a scientific worldview has evolved to become the norm, and the new language for describing our world is constantly changing. And, yet, the church continues to use an old language of sin and guilt, of earth down here and heaven up there, and of bloody sacrifice.

The old language may be called supernatural theism. "God is in his heaven, and all is right with the world," as the old saying goes. The old saying is incorrect. God is needed down in this world; this is where the problems are. According to supernatural theism, God intervenes, from time to time, to make corrections and to set thing straight. But does he do that? Ask those who have lost a loved one in this COVID-19 pandemic, for just one illustration. The image of God, "up" there in heaven, whatever or wherever that may be, can no longer be sustained. The portrayal of his Son as coming "down" to save us from ourselves, and then going back "up" to his heavenly home, makes no sense within our present cosmology. The language of our services of worship, however, is still grounded in supernatural theism. In the Book of Common Prayer of the Episcopal Church, the type of Sunday worship with which I am most familiar, the primary service of worship uses the words "death," "dying," and "sacrifice" some twenty times, when they are counted together. And much of the other language of angels and arch-angels, and even saints, without placing it in some context, tends to push God up and out of our world. The flat-world vocabulary of Sunday morning poorly communicates the faith of the church in a postmodern world. Decline in church membership and church attendance provide ample evidence for this claim. The language and images used in worship cannot take full blame. They do, though, show the most public face of Christian belief, and for that reason give us a place to begin.

The organization of this chapter falls into three categories: 1) affirmation rather than condemnation, 2) community rather than individuality, and 3) compassion rather than ceremony. Considering the first category, condemnation for sin receives too much emphasis. We are not, first of all and most of all, so guilty of sin that penitence should be the primary focus of worship. Nonetheless, on the Roman Catholic and Anglo Catholic end of the spectrum, in the Mass and the Eucharist, confession sets the tone. These services are thoroughly penitential, except for a brief hymn of praise: "Glory to God in the Highest." The death of Jesus, who on the cross shed his blood to save us, is the theological and liturgical heart of the service. When most of the Sundays of the year are Lenten, Easter Sunday feels like heresy. Because, as a celebration of new life, it appears out of step with the penitential norm. On the far Protestant end of the spectrum, we find the same message, but in sermons rather than liturgy.

The prosperity gospel is an exception to the traditional teaching of the church, but falls into the trap of blessing the materialistic consumerism of our culture. It preaches that financial blessings and physical well-being are God's will for everyone. Positive thinking and donating to the church are means to a person's material well-being. While that claim is questionable, pastors of large prosperity gospel churches have certainly realized a high degree of material well-being. They are some of the most prosperous of all pastors, ministers, and priests, living in grand homes and driving luxury vehicles. The prosperity gospel baptizes materialism and proposes to put the Holy Spirit to work serving our needs. It manages to ignore the Jesus of the Gospels, who said, "Foxes have their holes, the birds their roosts; but the Son of Man has nowhere to lay his head" (Matt 8:20 NEB). In the prosperity gospel, God is turned into a kind of Great Banker. The prosperity gospel manages to avoid guilt, but at the cost of perverting the message of the four Gospels.

The teachings of the church at large, moored in the language of sin, have made it very difficult for the individual person to avoid feelings of guilt, and at the same time have been very rewarding for the church. The church managed, unconsciously or by design, to assign guilt to a natural biological function, sex. In a stroke of genius, the church claimed the exclusive authority to forgive and assuage that guilt. I credit John Shelby Spong for making that point.[1] Guilt and forgiveness are the church's bread and butter. We are guilty by our birth, guilty for feeling normal human passions, guilty for not turning to the church, guilty for questioning the church, guilty, perhaps, for thinking.

However, the guilt and forgiveness doctrine no longer carries the weight it once did. We are, admittedly, terribly self-centered creatures who do much harm to each other and to our world. The Christian gospel, however, proclaims that God has already taken care of all that. Jesus, as the human face of God, revealed that God accepts us, cares about us, loves us, not for what we may become, but for what we are. St. Paul addressed this in Romans: "The conclusion of the matter is this: there is no condemnation for those who are united with Christ Jesus, because in Christ Jesus the life-giving law of the Spirit has set you free from the law of sin and death" (Rom 8:1 NEB). Condemnation and remorse are not the message of the gospel. The message is affirmation and the celebration of new life.

A great positive difference could be made by introducing a "Confession of Good Behavior" as part of Sunday worship. It could go something like this: "In this past week, Lord, because of your love and grace, I was able to [here name a specific act of compassion]." Transformation of the liturgies of the church is not the intention here. Rather, the purpose of this section of the chapter is to suggest that a more affirming and celebrative tone would be in keeping with the biblical message of Christ's victory over sin and death, and could thereby enhance the church's proclamation of the good news. The church overlooks what most of us know about raising a child. If we continually call the child a nasty little beast, he or she will most likely grow up to be a nasty big beast. We must temper the language of sin and guilt with the language of affirmation.

Considering the second category, Christianity has been corrupted by an extreme individualism. Emphasis on the value of the individual person

1. Spong, *Why Christianity Must Change or Die*, 90.

contributed to the strength of this country in its formative years. And the freedom to pursue individual achievement continues to further personal creativity. However, freedom is not free; freedom is laden with responsibility. A misunderstanding of freedom can lead to license and cause instability in a complex society. When the interest of the individual takes precedence over the needs of the community, both the individual and the community are damaged. The so-called me generation, those born between 1946 and 1964, comes to mind. The name derives from the self-involved narcissism associated with that generation. In truth, as we all suffer from some degree of self-involvement, every generation, to some extent, is a me generation.

In this postmodern world, a world of interaction and interdependence, of instant electronic communication, no person should act without reference to others. Within this matrix, we are formed and nurtured by the various communities in which we participate. These communities include family, a circle of friends, those with whom we work, and for many, the church.

The Bible reveals that the church should be thought of as a community. Our English word "church" is the translation of the Greek word *ekklesia* used in the New Testament. *Ekklesia* also gives us the English words "ecclesiastic" for members of the clergy, and "ecclesiastical" for things pertaining to the church. Jesus used the word *ekklesia* on only two occasions, both found in Matthew's Gospel. The most significant usage is in Jesus' praise of St. Peter: "And I say this to you: You are Peter, the Rock; and on this rock I will build my church, and the powers of death shall never conquer it" (Matt 16:18 NEB). There was no church at that time, but considering the meaning of the word *ekklesia*, Jesus' use of the word makes good sense. The word means "to call out." Jesus was speaking of those who are called out, summoned by God, to form a community of faith. The church is a community of people who have been called together to be a sign of God's presence.

We do not first live as individuals, and then develop relationships with others in community. The opposite is true. Relationships give us life and guide us in finding who we are as individual persons. It is within community that we become persons. It is within a community of faith that we become persons of faith. That is the power and purpose of community.

For example, St. Paul urges the Christians in Philippi to develop a healthy community spirit. "If then our common life in Christ yields anything to stir the heart, any loving consolation, any sharing of the Spirit, any warmth of affection or compassion, fill up my cup of happiness by thinking and feeling alike, with the same love for one another, the same turn of mind, and a common care for unity" (Phil 2:1–2 NEB).

His words ring more true now after churches have been closed for months, as members shelter at home to avoid catching and spreading the coronavirus that has caused a pandemic. Church services are being streamed electronically, and watched on cell phones and other electronic devices. The need to practice safe distancing has halted the gathering of church communities just as it has disrupted business and all personal social interactions.

The present hue and cry for a reopening of churches would appear to indicate that Christians, irrespective of denomination, are coming to realize the importance of their communities of faith. The more often heard cry, for personal freedom without regard for the welfare of others, is rooted in a misunderstanding. There is no freedom without responsibility. We are learning an important lesson from the disruption of community caused by this deadly virus, that we are better off together, in community. Every individual is responsible for the health of the community in which he or she lives. We are our brother's keeper, and our sister's, or we have no brothers and sisters. Sadly, it is also true that the mixture of a sense of entitlement with a willful ignorance has caused an aversion to collective action. What is occurring may be explained in terms developed by Robert N. Bellah and his co-authors. The point is made here that our language of self-understanding limits our ways of thinking and speaking. Using the terminology of the book, we would benefit from our "first language"[2] of individualism being expanded to include more regularly our "second language"[3] of social and communal responsibility.

Where the church is concerned, the faith of the community overshadows the faith of the individual. This is so because a community of persons can sustain a strong level of faith even as the faith of individual persons in the community wax and wane. For example, the Nicene Creed begins "We believe," expressing the faith of the community even as some individual members may be experiencing a "dry period." A "dry period" would be a time when doubts weigh against faith, making it difficult to recite the creed with full conviction. At such times the individual may lean on the community, which is able to speak from the overriding conviction of the many. This illustrates how the church can model the significance of community for all walks of life.

2. Bellah et al., *Habits of the Heart*, 20.

3. Bellah et al., *Habits of the Heart*, 157.

Considering the third category, without compassion all is lost. We Christians are not charged with protecting God, or his church, from those we consider the wrongheaded, misguided, perhaps dangerous other. We are charged with proclaiming, to all, the compassion of God. Too often we move to protect the institution from the very people it is called to serve. People are more important than rules. Jesus said it: "The Sabbath was made for the sake of man and not man for the Sabbath" (Mark 2:27 NEB). This is not an isolated example. Jesus also said, "Go learn what that text means, 'I require mercy, not sacrifice.' I did not come to invite virtuous people, but sinners" (Matt 9:13 NEB). With these statements, Jesus stands within the tradition of the prophets as they proclaimed a God who prefers compassion to ceremony. There are clear examples of this pronouncement, two of which are found in the writings of Amos and Micah. "I hate, I spurn your pilgrim-feasts; I will not delight in your sacred ceremonies. When you present your sacrifices and offerings I will not accept them, nor look on the buffaloes of your shared-offerings. Spare me the sound of your songs; I cannot endure the music of your lutes. Let justice roll on like a river and righteousness like an ever-flowing stream" (Amos 5:21–24 NEB). And: "God has told you what is good; and what is it that the Lord asks of you? Only to act justly, to love loyalty, to walk wisely before your God" (Mic 6:8 NEB). Viewed in the light of the Bible, ceremonies, religious rituals, cultic acts, are less important than our care for those who have been marginalized, dispossessed, impoverished by the culture in which they live. Church-established and supported soup kitchens, shelters, and food pantries indicate that it has heard and responded to this message. The sacrifice expected is the sacrifice of ourselves, making compassion a central act of worship.

Christ is best known by persons within a community of faith, where people find affirmation and experience compassion. Then, by speaking these truths in the language of the time, the public face of the church will become a recognizable face of Christ for Sunday, and for all other days of the week.

[handwritten margin note: Then why would God need Jesus to be sacrificed?]

SIDEBAR

Prayer

PRAYER BECOMES A PROBLEM when we are worshiping a God who does not intervene at our request or in response to our religious ceremonies. The providence of God provides clarification for this problem with prayer because the two aspects of providence, general and special, make helpful distinctions. General providence speaks of God's care of all creation, his maintenance of the natural order. His uninterrupted creative energy and purpose fall within the category of general providence. Special providence is God's particular care for his church and its people.

Special providence is the problematic area for prayer. Prayer that asks for special intervention in our affairs is based on the false assumption that we can activate God's special providence. Such prayer, formulated as asking, and then waiting for an answer of yes, no, or later, has lost its way. Our prayers must be more than asking favors of God. Because Christianity is a matter of relationships, prayer becomes the language of relationships. It is the communication needed to maintain a healthy relationship with God.

Within general providence there is no difficulty with prayer so long as it is offered as a way of aligning ourselves with God's love and his care for creation. Prayer, at its best, opens us and exposes us to God's presence throughout our world and our lives. By our prayers, we join ourselves to God. In our prayers, we listen for his invitation into a relationship offered through the Spirit to our spirit. Prayer is conversation.

The Lord's Prayer fits into this definition of prayer as the conversation of relationship. Addressing God as "Father," with no religious prelude of praise or accommodation, implies a relationship already in existence. A few words of praise do follow, and lead to the first petition, "thy kingdom come," which is not so much a request as a move to align us with God's goal for his world. From that general petition, we move to a petition for food, but only for the bare minimum, only for what is needed to survive the day. The next petition, by its length and by its central position, and as the only place where our participation is invoked, stands out as the heart of the prayer. "Forgive us the wrong we have done, as we forgive those who have wronged us" (Matt 6:12 NEB). Forgiveness is the heart and soul of relationships, of the life, death, and resurrection of Jesus, of the Christian faith, of the life of the world. Then, the Lord's Prayer ends, "Do not bring us to the test" (Matt 6:13a and Luke 11:4b NEB). A succession of tests, trials, and temptations are a part of life in general. General providence provides a better fit for the Lord's Prayer than does special providence. That fit moves the prayer away from being petitions for God's intervention and toward its being a prayer for our relationship with God for the sake of this world.

When we turn to special providence, there are two parables that could be mistakenly interpreted to mean that God will intervene in our affairs if we can only be brazen enough and persistent enough. The parable of the late-night friend tells of a friend arriving in the middle of the night to borrow three loaves of bread because he has an unexpected houseguest. At first, he is turned away, but eventually he succeeds, and his friend gets up to give him the loaves. This parable introduces the saying of Jesus, "ask, and you will receive; seek and you will find; knock and the door will be opened" (Luke 11:10 NEB). Then follows the saying, "If you, then, as bad as you are, know how to give your children what is good for them, how much more will the heavenly Father give the Holy Spirit to those who ask him" (Luke 11:13 NEB). Realizing that the words about "getting up" are words of resurrection, and seeing that the ultimate gift is the Spirit, this section of Luke's Gospel is not about persistence in prayer to get God's attention. This parable is about the full grace of God made available by the life, death, and resurrection of Jesus. Grace is God's gift to us of himself. He need not intervene because he is with us fully and completely in his Spirit.

The second parable is that of the unjust judge. It is somewhat surprising that Jesus would portray God as an unjust judge, but that is how he makes his point that the judge's disposition, not the widow's persistence, is the message of the parable. The judge says to himself, "I will see her righted before she wears me out with her persistence" (Luke 18:5b NEB). The unjust judge is bemoaning his situation, with no regard for the widow's plight. It is not her just cause, nor her persistence, which prevails. The unjust judge, a representation of God, is motivated by his own cares. The parable is about God's grace, not our success at prayer.

Taken one step further, we learn that prayer is not our job. "We do not even know how we ought to pray, but through our inarticulate groans the Spirit himself is pleading for us, and God who searches our inmost being knows what the Spirit means, because he pleads for God's people in God's own way" (Rom 8:26b–27 NEB). The Spirit prays for us and in us. The Spirit takes care to bring us together in a living relationship. Our part is to let the Spirit's energy flow between us and herself, in prayer that is the language of relations, not imploring, but conversing.

17

Christianity and Religion

I DON'T BELIEVE CHRISTIANITY is a religion. To clarify that statement, more needs to be said about both Christianity and religion. Religion is what we humans have used to get the deity, or deities, to be on our side. The purpose of religion is to appease, even manipulate the god or gods. Religion was used, and is still used, to persuade God to give us a successful hunt, a plentiful harvest, a more lucrative business deal, a healthier and happier life. As religion is practiced to earn God's acceptance, Christianity celebrates our having already received God's acceptance. The claim of Christianity is that we do not need to bring God around, to persuade him to look upon us favorably. We already have in our possession all that religion proposes to negotiate for us.

Jesus' parable of the prodigal son, which should be called the parable of the loving father, is a story of God's ready acceptance. After squandering his inheritance, the wayward son sees that his only option is to return home and throw himself upon his father's mercy. As he travels toward home, he rehearses his excuses. When he was still a distance from home, his father saw him and ran to him with open arms. Before the son could say a word, make excuses, beg for forgiveness, his father kissed him and began to make plans for a party to celebrate his return. "But when he was still a long way off his father saw him, and his heart went out to him" (Luke 15:20 NEB). The life of Jesus was a demonstration of God's love and acceptance shown by the father in this parable. Jesus' readiness to sit and eat with those considered outcasts, sinners, undesirables, is a clear and broad revelation of God's acceptance of all. God requires no prompting from us, no religious negotiations. Christianity is the expression and celebration of that good news, and the end of religion.

Our failure to understand the nonreligious nature of Christianity is one cause of the decline in church membership and attendance. Various polls, including one by the Pew Research Center, found that about one quarter of those surveyed consider themselves spiritual but not religious. The church's determination to be a religion sets it up to be included in this growing rejection. The church, as organized religion, has become too in- flexible, too opposed to questions, and too wary of an open faith. Histori- cally, the church as a body has tended to be anti-intellectual, has tended to reject science, has questioned women's rights, and has been, generally, rather narrow minded. The church's reaction to the culture's rejection of its religious features is to become a more rigid religious organization by tight- ening its rules and regulations concerning who is in and who is out. But a church that closes ranks in the face of change is not a Christian church.

It is no wonder that people are turned off by what they perceive to be a religion of external concerns, too much like any other worldly organiza- tion. According to Diana Butler Bass, the statement, "I am spiritual, but not religious" is a way of saying, "I am unhappy with the church as an expression of my faith, and I am unhappy with the church as a way of practicing my faith."[1] It is to say, "I am looking for another way to connect with God, or a Higher Power, or something that can give my life more meaning." Many people hunger for something more than an individualistic materialism, a life built on consumerism, on acquiring more stuff. Spirituality, by contrast, is an internal and more positive avenue to a more human and purposeful life.

There is, though, the risk of trying to become too spiritual. Remember the old warning: "Don't become so heavenly minded that you are of no earthly good."

Christianity is a very down-to-earth way of responding to God. The incarnation, discussed in chapter 7, shows that God is very comfortable with revealing himself in and through an earthy human being. Jesus was the face of God, not despite his humanity but through his humanity. And Jesus was an unwashed itinerant preacher who traveled around with a small band of everyday folk in a rural part of his country. In his teachings, he said more about money than he did about prayer. During his very short public

1. Bass, *Christianity after Religion*, 68.

ministry, one year long, perhaps as many as three years, nothing that he did was significantly religious. The resurrection was not a religious event. It occurred outside the bounds of religion. The attempt, by some, to be more spiritual than Jesus is fraught with as many problems as trying to shore up a rejected religion by making it more religious.

The confusion of Christianity with religion, and an oblique attempt at spirituality, is seen in the movies that have come out of Hollywood for many years. And movies reflect the culture. My first two examples are dated but illustrate the confusion by making the point that religious movies are seldom Christian, and Christian movies are seldom religious. The two examples are *The Robe* and *Hombre*. Because they are old movies, I will offer a summary of each story as I draw from them the point I wish to make.

The Robe, based on the novel by Lloyd C. Douglas, was released in 1953. It was a highly popular movie of the grand religious genre. The story is that of a dissolute Roman tribune, Marcus Gallio, played by Richard Burton. As a tribune stationed in Jerusalem, he was assigned to carry out the crucifixion of Jesus. Following the crucifixion, he won Jesus' robe in a dice game. This much of the story is biblically based, but follows the more elaborate version of the crucifixion in John's Gospel: "The soldiers, having crucified Jesus, took possession of his clothes, and divided them into four parts, one for each soldier, leaving out the tunic. The tunic was seamless, woven in one piece throughout; so, they said to one another, 'We must not tear this; let us toss for it'" (John 19:23–24a NEB). The earlier biblical account, in Mark's Gospel, is very brief. "They divided his clothes among them, casting lots to decide what each would have" (Mark 15:24b NEB).

The movie, drawing upon the embellished version, is the story of the effect of Jesus' tunic, or robe, on Marcus Gallio, its owner by the toss of the dice. Soon after taking possession of the robe, he begins to have disturbing dreams, and then a feeling of guilt about the part he took in the crucifixion. The robe, he comes to believe, is the cause of his problems, and he decides to destroy it. Enter Demetrius, played by Victor Mature, a slave owned by Marcus Gallio. Demetrius escapes with the robe, thereby saving it from destruction. In the course of his efforts to find his slave and regain possession of the robe, Marcus Gallio learns more about Jesus, the man he crucified, and he is converted to Christianity. This is a biblical epic about a magic cape, and how a man is brought to faith in Jesus by its miraculous effect upon him. If Christian at all, this religious movie is so at the most simplistic level.

Hombre, based on the novel by Elmore Leonard, was released in 1967. It is a typical Western, set in Arizona in the 1880s. John Russell, played by Paul Newman, is a white man who has been raised by a band of Apache Indians. He is returning to Arizona to collect an inheritance when the stagecoach he is traveling in is attacked by a band of outlaws led by Cicero Grimes, played by Richard Boone. Among the passengers on the stagecoach are an Indian Agent, Professor Favor, and his wife. The outlaws know that Favor is carrying money he stole from the very Apaches that Russell grew up with. Grimes and his outlaws manage to take Mrs. Favor hostage, and they stake her out in the sun to persuade Professor Favor to turn the money over to them. He refuses to part with his money, and, in any case, it appears that Mrs. Favor is bait in a trap. Russell, who had withdrawn into his Apache way of life, realizes that he is the only one who has any chance of saving Mrs. Favor. Looking at her, and the agony she is enduring, Russell's Christian faith reasserts itself. He makes plans to rescue her, but he does not fully succeed. She is rescued, but he is left exposed to the outlaws. Russell and Grimes kill each other in a final shoot-out. Russell gives his life to save Mrs. Favor, a strongly Christian act that is the climax of a completely nonreligious movie. Though somewhat out of date, these two stories illustrate the Christianity-and-religion confusion in our culture.

More recent movies seem to have little understanding or concern for religion or Christianity, perhaps because of the growing number of persons who claim to be spiritual but not religious and have no affiliation with any Christian church. Consciously or unconsciously, more recent movies address a spiritual yearning for something more than this small world of our confinement. The Star Wars movies, with the great success of *The Empire Strikes Back,* released in 1980, would itself be dated if not for the many sequels. It is an interesting mixture of science fiction and mysticism. The greeting, "May the force be with you," sums up the mysticism of the movie, and speaks to our spiritual emptiness.

A more recent movie that mixes science fiction with fantasy is *Avatar,* released in 2009. It, too, attempts to touch our spiritual emptiness, our desire to find something more than our culture offers, and has been spoken of as a religious film. The need for someone larger than life, more powerful and able to face what we must face, is certainly the appeal of the more than twenty Marvel movies. These movies give us comic book men and women with superhero powers who come to the rescue of our world. The Harry Potter movies are magic in themselves, holding open to us a door into a parallel world of wizards, beasts, and a cosmic battle between the forces of good and evil. It is not my intention to disparage any of these movies. They are good entertainment, and I have enjoyed many of them. They do, though, illustrate and mirror back to us our often-confused yearnings for a life with more depth of purposes, hope, and joy. They show a faulty understanding of Christianity and religion but do offer a brief escape from a world that is too small when we think this is all there is.

In contrast to the doubt expressed in our culture, there is the confidence of St. Paul: "Christ died for us while we were yet sinners, and that is God's own proof of his love towards us" (Rom 5:8b NEB). The initiative is God's: accepting, inviting, caring. In St. Paul's thoughts, no religious observance of Jewish law was a prerequisite to God's love. No dietary regulations, no recognition of feast days, no efforts at purity were required, only trust in God. For St. Paul, the good news that completely altered his life was the God he saw in the life of Jesus. And, that life was lived and offered before we could in any way claim to be right with God. All we need do is accept our acceptance. The preemptive actions of God in Jesus put an end to religion.

St. Paul was convinced that God had solved his problems with us independently of what we are doing, or not doing. The Christian church struggles with St. Paul. It has spent two thousand years trying to avoid, circumvent, or redefine him. The approach of the church has been to consider it unfair, outrageous, and by God wrong of God, not to demand more from us. At the least, God should require that we learn, and obey to the letter, the Ten Commandments, even though Jesus seldom mentioned them. So, if God will not require a more demanding religion, we will. However, Christianity is not a religion of rules and regulations, of discipline and law. They are too easily used for control and exclusion. They are desired because they give us a way to measure ourselves against one another, a way of determining who is a winner and who is a loser. If Christianity is to survive, it must be more than a religion. It must revolve around and within a relationship of trust and love. Relationships thrive on mutual trust, forgiveness, and a flexible give-and-take. Religion, with all its dos and don'ts, destroys relationships, and destroys Christianity because Christianity is a matter of relationships.

The Christian church does use the accoutrements of religion: vestments, music, and ceremonies that involve rituals. It celebrates special times and days. Even the nonliturgical churches have sufficient form to allow members to know what will come next in a service of worship. The features of religion are certainly used, but ritual observances do not make Christianity a religion. They are not used to importune but to celebrate.

In the Episcopal Church, we speak of celebrating the Eucharist, or Holy Communion, or the Mass. I have been involved in the practice of religion for half a century, having been ordained to the priesthood on June 1, 1963. From that date to this time in early 2022, I have conducted services of worship on too many Sundays to count, baptized many, performed innumerable marriages, and buried too many. During this COVID-19 pandemic, circumstances are very different and even difficult. The days go slowly by while the weeks pass quickly. There seem to be no named days of the week, but only today, yesterday, and the next day to come. In an attempt to control the spread of the virus, Episcopal churches were closed, making Sunday the most peculiar day in the week for me. I have not been to church on a Sunday for many weeks. Services are being streamed, and watched on computers, cell phones, and tablets. That is better than nothing, and I commend those who are working so hard to make this electronic worship available. Much is lost, however, when we are sheltering in place and unable to interact with others during the service. Worship by watching a screen is never fully satisfying. Christianity is not a spectator sport. Faith, at some point, becomes what we do.

While living in a time of pandemic, we cannot do religious services very well, but at any time we can do Christianity. We can telephone a friend or family member. We can Skype, tweet, go on Facebook. We can send an email. We can reach out, show that we have not forgotten, that we care and are concerned. It is not at all adequate. Thanks to our technology, though, we can reach far beyond the six feet of distancing that is recommended. One thing that has become clear to me in these dreadful circumstances is that religion is what we do for ourselves; Christianity is what we do with and for another person.

Christianity, as I have said, is a matter of relationships, not only with God, but also with other persons. We do, though, find relationships difficult. We can get angry with a friend, become estranged from a son or daughter, stop speaking to a sister or brother, often for no good reason, or for a reason we no longer remember. The good news, the gospel, is that God accepts us into our relationship with him, to quote an old hymn, "Just as I am, without one plea." We are good, basically, and do not need to make a plea for acceptance. God is offering a fully restored relationship, an irrevocable relationship. It is something like a marriage, to borrow an analogy from Capon. God takes us "For better for worse, for richer for poorer, in sickness and health, to love and cherish."[2] We need only respond, "I do," but with the realization that the relationship will include a lot of other people. God's love for us embraces everyone. If, by the grace of God, we are loved and accepted, there is no purpose in religion, except for celebration.

2. Capon, *Mystery of Christ*, 66.

SIDEBAR

Connecting

WHAT LITTLE VALUE RELIGION may have is that it serves to remind us that our relationship with God is badly flawed. Our attempts to appease God indicate our awareness that we are not living as we should in relationship to him or to anyone else. We live disconnected, out of touch to the extent that electronic dating services are finding a place in our culture. Religion is one activity that helps make us aware of our disconnects.

The root meaning of the word "religion" points to its relevance in this plight. Behind our English word is the Latin word *religio*. *Ligio* is the basis for our word's ligament and ligature, and means to bind, to tie together, to connect. Religion is not, though, our means of reconnecting with God, but an aid in our celebrating the reconnection already secured.

St. Paul is clear on this: "When anyone is united to Christ there is a new world; the old order has gone, and a new order has already begun. From first to last this has been the work of God. He has reconciled us men to himself through Christ, and he has enlisted us in this service of reconciliation. What I mean is, that God was in Christ reconciling the world to himself, no longer holding men's misdeeds against them, and that he has entrusted us with the message of reconciliation" (2 Cor 5:17–19 NEB). Much is said in this passage. God has taken the initiative to reconcile us to himself, shaping a personal reconnection of such significance and strength that we are now enlisted in its furtherance. "Furtherance" is an appropriate word because St. Paul was not inventing a new religion, nor, for that matter, was Jesus.

Jesus appeared to believe that his vocation was to fulfill, in his own life, the purpose of God's covenant with Israel. Israel was to be the people through whom the whole world was to be blessed with new life. In the theology of St. Paul, Jesus, by his death and resurrection, had succeeded in fulfilling Israel's purpose in the plan of God. St. Paul believed that his vocation was to proclaim the victory of Jesus.

The task of Christianity is to proclaim the new way of being human that was made possible by the life and death of Jesus. It is a way of compassion rather than ceremony. It is a way of hope and celebration that may use the features of religion but is not a religion. Religion is our attempt to grasp God; Christianity is our celebration of being grasped by God.

18

Why and Who

I DON'T BELIEVE WE ask the right questions. We ask "Why?" questions. God gives "Who!" answers. Who is the answer. There is no question mark at the end of the previous sentence because it is not a question. It is a statement. We ask, "Why did it happen? Why me?" God answers, "Here I am. I am the one who has been with you all along." We miss his answer and fail to know his presence because asking the wrong question predisposes us to listen for the wrong answer. Or, we simply fail to listen.

God assures us that he is the one who is with us, but he does not explain himself. In the story of Moses encountering God in a burning bush that is not consumed, God never explains what is happening to the bush. He says no more to Moses than, "I will be what I will be," and you are the one who will go to Egypt for me (Exod 3). A pastoral element can be heard when the name of God is translated, "I will be what I will be," rather than "I Am." That alternative translation can mean whatever difficulties you encounter, I will be who you need me to be in that situation. But, God does not say why.

No explanation is offered because explanations give little comfort. Being told that the person who smashed into the side of your car was intoxicated, or texting, does not make the situation any better. Now you know why the accident happened, but the explanation may only make you angrier. Likewise, knowing why your house burned down, or was blown and washed away, offers little consolation. As I think back to Hurricane

Part VI: Now

Katrina in August of 2005, I could have asked, "Why me, Lord? I'm really a good guy, why did I lose my home? Why did my brother have to die in the storm?" Those were major, tragic events to work through, both in mind and feelings, and in simply going forward from day to day. I had many questions, but my experience was that learning about barometric pressure, about millibars, about guiding air currents and water temperature, did not in any way help me feel any better or handle the hurricane with more aplomb. No matter if we experience an accident, an illness, a natural disaster, or a pandemic, explanations of why afford little comfort.

Who was with me at the time, though, sharing the danger and the loss, provided a way through the pain and made a difference. One incident stands out in my memory. It was rumored that cell phones would work at the foot of the Highway 90 Bridge over the Bay of St. Louis between the towns of Bay St. Louis and Pass Christian. The bridge had been destroyed by the hurricane, so it was to our end of the downed bridge that my wife and I went to try to call our son in Houston. We needed to let him know that we were alive and unhurt. My phone did not work, not here, or there, or anywhere around the foot of the bridge. My frustration was mounting when I saw a cousin's young son walking along having a conversation with one of his sisters on his cell phone. I grabbed him and implored him to get a message to our son through his sister. The message went out: from me to the young cousin, to his sister, to our son, that his parents were dirty, tired, disheartened, but well enough under the circumstances. A string of people who were willing to stand in as a solution to our problem accomplished putting our minds at ease, and our son's. They represented God's presence while we were coping with the disaster.

Those who stand with us make it bearable when there is no electricity, no running water, no grocery store, no drug store, no gas station, none of those things we normally take for granted. Who is with us at such a time can make all the difference in the world. Those who are with us, in good times and in bad, are crucial to how we enjoy or how we endure an experience. Trust that God is also with us is equally crucial to our sense of well-being, our feeling of hope.

Not only, though, do we too often ask the wrong question, too often we also prove ourselves to be poor listeners. We Americans are a noisy people. Think of the cars in traffic around us with the sound systems cranked up to full volume. They can be heard six cars away even when our windows are up and our air conditioning running. My home offers another example. I live the equivalent of six blocks from a couple of bar/restaurants, but the bands that play on weekend nights can be clearly heard in my home, again with the windows closed and the air conditioning running. Our clamor makes it difficult for us to find one another, much less find a God who is silently present.

"'Go out and stand before me on top of the mountain,' the Lord said to him [Elijah]. Then the Lord passed by and sent a furious wind that split the hills and shattered the rocks—but the Lord was not in the wind. The wind stopped blowing, and then there was an earthquake—but the Lord was not in the earthquake. After the earthquake there was a fire—but the Lord was not in the fire. And after the fire there was the soft whisper of a voice. When Elijah heard it, he covered his face" (1 Kgs 19:11–12 GN). In the King James Version of the Bible, which may be better known to some, "after the fire a still small voice." The New Revised Standard Version of the Bible has the better translation for our purpose: "after the fire a sound of sheer silence." God is with us in "sheer silence," present without sound, word, or explanation.

There are, of course, words, many words, but words spoken through some person, prophet as a spokesperson, evangelist through his gospel, preacher from the pulpit, and, ultimately, in the parables of Jesus. Dr. Seuss provides a more recent approach, if somewhat whimsical, by putting faith into words for children. *How the Grinch Stole Christmas* sorts things out quite well. The Grinch, as some of you will know, sneaked into Whoville and stole all the Christmas decorations and gifts. He even took the roast beast, a dastardly thing to do. But, afterwards, what the Grinch heard came as a surprise, "But the sound wasn't *sad!* Why, this sound was merry!"[1]

Commercialism has bent Christmas out of recognition. And political correctness, changing Christmas to holiday (not realizing the root meaning of holiday is holy day) has added another twist. Lip service is still given to who it is all about, but the great emphasis is on stuff. Purchasing stuff, giving stuff, and receiving stuff drowns out the real words. "*Then* the Grinch thought of something he hadn't before. 'Maybe Christmas,' he thought, '*doesn't* come from a store.'"[2] Even so, all the "whos" get shuffled about, the who of Christmas and of Christianity, the Whos of Whoville, and each of us, whoever we are.

1. Dr. Seuss, *How the Grinch Stole Christmas.*
2. Dr. Seuss, *How the Grinch Stole Christmas.*

What the Grinch did not at first know, but the Whos of Whoville did know, and what we know, though it is impossible to explain, is that Jesus is "The Who"! God took the initiative, not in explaining why, but in offering a person, Jesus, the Who of God.

At all levels, persons with us are better than answers for us. COVID-19 drives that truth home in a tragic way, as people die in hospitals separated from their loved ones. Spouses, parents, children, and friends are kept out, kept away. It is painful to all: patients, family and friends, and even to those in the medical profession. COVID-19 awakens, in those of us who have any feelings, our very human need to be with our loved ones, to have them with us in tragic times as well as in happy times. In all circumstances, who is with us, and who we are with, is of the highest importance.

As stated before, Jesus is the Who of God, but who knew it? St. Peter, perhaps, was the first who understood this vital truth. The story labeled the Confession of Peter is found in all the first three Gospels. Jesus and his disciples were on the road again when he asked them, "Who do men say I am?" (Mark 8:27b NEB). The disciples answered that there was a bit of confusion, with some saying he might be John the Baptist, others saying he could be Elijah or one of the other prophets. "'And you,' he asked, 'Who do you say I am?' Peter replied: 'You are the Messiah'" (Mark 8:29 NEB). Only in Matthew's Gospel (16:18) do we find the verse in which Peter is acclaimed the rock on which Jesus will build his church. With or without that verse, this interchange took place among regular people here on this earth, as Jesus and his companions were walking toward a group of villages north of Galilee. It was an early religious poll, of sorts. Jesus was checking up on the success of his message. The job of puzzling out who Jesus is began then and continues now, among us, as we journey through life, trying to understand and preserve our relationships with God and with one another. Such questions are natural.

Jesus evidently had questions. The disciples must surely have had questions. Most people today have questions. Our questions are driven by a desire to know, by curiosity, and by doubt. I once found an amazingly theological message in a fortune cookie: "I give you doubt to prove that there is faith." Many who attend church have doubts and are looking for answers. People have approached me at church, as would be expected, but also, unexpectedly, at dinner parties, while traveling on a plane, and in the Mockingbird Café a few blocks from my home. At the Bay-Waveland Yacht Club, where I am a past commodore and the fleet chaplain, I have been approached with questions in the bar and even while out on a sailboat. Very few people with whom I have had any interaction, or even just a conversation, have failed, eventually, to ask a question about some aspect of the Bible or the Christian faith. That is true of some who admit to having no religious beliefs at all. And now, the COVID-19 pandemic is provoking many questions, most of which are why question that have been asked before, over and over again. Now, though, they are asked with more urgency.

"Who" is the answer, but not the answer we get when we ask "Why?" Who is Christianity all about? Who am I if I believe, if I do not believe? Those are better questions. Focusing on who, rather than on why, takes us further into the relationships of a good life. Christianity, and life itself, are about persons, other persons, and the person of Christ. Deep down within ourselves we know that who is more important than why. It is Jesus who showed us the "who" of God.

SIDEBAR

Who

JESUS IS ACCEPTED AS the "Who of God" throughout the Christian church. Expressed more traditionally, Jesus is the clearest revelation and demonstration of God. As a man of his own time, Jesus gives us our most clear revelation of who God is, of what he is like.

Jesus' revelation of God is expressed at two places in John's Gospel: "No one has ever seen God; but God's only Son, he who is nearest to the Father's heart, he has made him known" (1:18, NEB). And, "Anyone who has seen me [Jesus] has seen the Father" (14:9b NEB). These two blunt statements, though very much to the point, fail to acknowledge the mystery we encounter when considering the revelation of the Father in the life of the Son.

The mystery is extended by Jesus' chosen mode of teaching. He used parables, and parables are ambiguous by design. At the most basic level, a parable makes its point by putting one thing alongside another. A parable's strength lies in the nature of the comparison, and Jesus often stretched the comparison, as when he likened God to an unjust judge (Luke 18:2–8). Some of the parables of Jesus are very brief, of only one line, as when he said, "People who are well do not need a doctor, but only those who are sick" (Mark 2:17 GN). His better-known parables are little stories that challenge our imagination, and sometimes confuse us. An example of the confusion is the misnaming of the parable of the prodigal son. The central figure is not the wayward son but the loving father who forgave him. Another parable open to various interpretations is the parable of the good Samaritan. "A man was on his way from Jerusalem down to Jericho when he fell in with robbers, who stripped him, beat him, and went off leaving him half dead" (Luke 10:30 NEB). Various people passed by who could have helped him but did not. "But a Samaritan who was making the journey came upon him, and when he saw him was moved to pity" (Luke 10:33 NEB). There were only ill feelings between Jews and Samaritans, but even so, it was the Samaritan who came to the rescue. Here I follow the interpretation of Robert Farrar Capon. He proposes that the Christ figure in the parable is not the Samaritan, but the injured man.[1] Jesus suffered everyone's misunderstanding, the denial of his closest companions, and an agonizing, painful death by crucifixion. He, like the man set upon by robbers, is the victim. Capon's position on the parable of the good Samaritan is supported by the church's identification of Jesus as the suffering servant.

Very early in the development of Christianity, the Servant Songs of the prophet Isaiah were adopted as explanations of the life and death of Jesus. There are four Servant Songs: Isaiah 42:1–4; 49:1–6; 50:4–11; and 52:13–53:12. The passage most often applied to Jesus is from the fourth Servant Song, "Yet on himself he bore our sufferings, our torments he endured, while we counted him smitten by God, struck down by disease and misery; but he was pierced for our transgressions, tortured for our iniquities; the chastisement he bore is health for us and by his scourging we are healed" (Isa 53:4–5 NEB). Our relationships are defined, according to Capon, by the one who was present in human history as the victim, Jesus of Nazareth.

In the writings of Isaiah, the suffering servant is Israel. Even so, Jesus was quickly identified with the suffering servant. It is likely that the identification came about because Jesus himself believed he was assuming the role of Israel in the redemption of the world, and he saw that fulfilling that role would entail suffering.

Following the evidence found in Isaiah, in the parable of the good Samaritan, in the crucifixion, the unavoidable conclusion is that the God revealed by Jesus is a God who suffers with us. God does not tamper with us, or with the world around us. He does not alter the shape or the direction of life other than by his loving presence in all that befalls us. God suffers with us, and he rejoices with us, so closely that we are unaware of his presence. That is the way of God, and that is who God is.

---

1. Capon, *Kingdom, Grace, Judgment*, 212.

Conclusion

This project, which has absorbed me for over six years, has been very satisfying. I have figured out what I don't believe, and in the process, what I do believe. The chapters have evolved through the writing process. I have had to write one or two chapters before I could determine what the subject of the next one should be.

Throughout, I have been guided by what Robert Farrar Capon wrote: "As I said, the theologian's real work is not to prove that the faith is true, only that it's interesting."[1] I have made no attempt to prove the existence of God, but I have attempted to address the importance of his immanence. Also, I have accepted Holy Scripture as foundational, not as prooftexts, though, but as illustrations. And I find that I have consistently turned to the Bible for support. Our experiences in life and the experiences recorded in the Bible often reinforce each other when the Bible is taken seriously rather than literally. I subscribe to the saying: "It (whatever it may be) is not true because it is in the Bible, it is in the Bible because it is true." Hopefully, some will find this book true and interesting.

There are three passages in the New Testament I perceive to be elemental, and I turn to them now in my conclusion. One is the Great Commandment, found in the following passages: Mark 12:2–31; Luke 10:25–28; and Matthew 22:34–40. For his Great Commandment, Jesus drew upon his heritage as an Israelite. The first part of the Great Commandment is, "Hear, O Israel, the Lord is our God, one Lord, and you must love the Lord your God with all your heart and soul and strength" (Deut 6:46 NEB). The second part is, "You shall not seek revenge, or cherish anger towards your kinsfolk; you shall love your neighbor as a man like yourself. I am the Lord"

1. Capon, *Romance of the Word*, 309.

(Lev 19:18 NEB). When Jesus was asked of all the commandments, which is first, he combined the passages from Deuteronomy and Leviticus to produce his summary of the Law.

I have devoted additional space to the Great Commandment, risking repetition, because I consider it the key to understanding Holy Scripture. Any passage that fails to align with it, or is in any way contradictory, must be studied with great care. It is the window through which all other passages are to be seen, approached, and evaluated. It provides our way of seeing all of Scripture.

The second passage of significant importance is the story of Jesus and Zacchaeus. This story is the gospel in miniature. Zacchaeus was a rich tax collector in Jericho, a city just north of Jerusalem. Tax collectors were generally despised, not only for being dishonest, but for collaborating with the enemy, Rome. The Roman general, Pompey, had conquered most of the area in 64 BCE. A tax collector, such as Zacchaeus, would have entered a contract with the Roman authorities for the right to collect revenues.

Evidently, Zacchaeus had heard that Jesus was to pass nearby, and he wanted very much to see him. He was interested enough to risk going into an unfriendly crowd. Not only was he disliked, but also very short, which put his nose dangerously close to elbow height. He could not see over the crowd, so he climbed up into a tree in order to see Jesus pass by. Jesus looked up, saw him in the tree, and invited himself to Zacchaeus's home. Zacchaeus hoped for a glimpse and got a house guest. There was the usual grumble of disapproval because Jesus was once again going to eat with a sinner. How could a tax collector, in cahoots with the hated Roman overlords, not be a sinner (Luke 19:1–9)?

Here, the story becomes the gospel in miniature. Jesus accepts Zacchaeus just as he is, a crooked little tax collector up a tree. Jesus did not first ask Zacchaeus to repent and make reparations. Jesus saw him, reached out to him, and called him down out of the tree. All of this came before Zacchaeus said a word or made a move toward changing his ways. All Zacchaeus had to do was accept his acceptance. Zacchaeus did just that. After meeting Jesus, he declared that he would now give half his possessions to the poor and repay those whom he had cheated. These reparations were not offered to gain Jesus' acceptance. Zacchaeus knew already that he was accepted. He was a new person, responding to what he had received. He had been lost, but now was found, given new life in Christ, and it was good news. This story is a summary of what we may experience.

The third passage of particular interest is the parable of the nations. The most significant verses in the parable are those in which we are told that anything we do for another person, no matter how unimportant he or she may be, we are doing for the Lord (Matt 25:31–46). And, in reverse, what we fail to do for another, we fail to do for the Lord. Our interactions and relationships with God and one another cannot be separated; they are inextricably intertwined. It is unproductive to get into a "chicken or egg" discussion concerning which relationship must come first. Our relationship with God and our relationships with others are mysteriously dependent upon each other. In this parable we are guided in what to do.

I return to Capon: "Theology is not, as the old manuals had it, 'the science of God and things divine'; properly speaking, it is not about God but about the mystery of God's relationship to the world."[2] Christianity, as I have stated more than once, is a matter of relationships.

The mystery of God's relation to the world becomes a problem of broader concern in troubled times, as in a hurricane, in an earthquake or forest fire, and in a pandemic. In such times, our relationship with a loving Father God is difficult to reconcile with what we experience as a heartless Mother Nature. This disparity between God's love and nature's heartlessness expresses the tension between Christianity and science. Denying science is no solution, whether it be in rejecting climate change or ignoring medical advice during a pandemic. Defending Holy Scripture by claiming scientific fact where clearly it is not factual or scientific is also no solution.

A theology needs to be developed that incorporates science. Modern science and theology are observing the same reality. Father God is forgiving, but Mother Nature is not. On the surface, this does seem to be an accurate description, which makes it easy to separate God and nature. Our frightening world of dangerous freedoms is, nonetheless, the natural world inhabited by God. And though we wish it to be otherwise, he saves us in this world, not from it. Following Jesus is not about getting into heaven, but about getting with our neighbors and making life here better. Eternal life cannot be defined in terms of time, it is outside of time. Eternal life must be defined in terms of quality, particularly in the quality of our relationships. Heaven and hell are qualities of life, not qualities of death. Those two words, heaven and hell, describe qualities that begin in the here and now. Following Jesus does not remove us from the natural course of life. Theology looks at the life of Jesus and sees that he had to go through the

2. Capon, *Romance of the Word*, 277.

cross to get to Easter. By analogy, Good Friday is heartless Mother Nature and Easter Sunday is loving Father God. Jesus expressed this simply, if
cryptically, in each of the first three Gospels: "For if you want to save your
own life, you will lose it, but if you lose your life for my sake, you will save
it" (Luke 9:24 GN). When we avoid Good Friday, we will not find Easter
Sunday. It is all a great big wonderful messy organism that neither theology
nor science can fully command. Perhaps, though, in navigating nature we
will find ourselves in the presence of God.

Sailing is good training for navigating nature and for listening for God.
In a power boat we barge through (too much the American way) without
regard to wind or water. Sailing, though, requires cooperation with nature.
In a sailboat, we must work with the wind, the tides, and the currents. There
is no other way in a sailboat. In the present pandemic, distancing, wearing
a mask, washing one's hands are simple ways of accommodating Mother
Nature. Refusing to accept these necessities, for whatever reason, is an attempt to power through. Powering through has never worked.

A simple truism is that we cannot break the laws of nature. Gravity, for
instance, is a law we cannot break; it will break us. Science, by its approach
to nature, has brought immense improvements to our quality of life. Jesus'
Great Commandment, perhaps, can also be understood as a law of nature
that has brought immense improvements to our quality of life. We may
think we can break it and escape unscathed, but we cannot. This would be
a better world if we brought the same attitude to bear in dealing with the
ways of God that we bring to obeying the laws of nature.

When I began this book, we were in what is being called "normal time,"
in contrast with what is now called our "new normal." It may be new, but it
is anything but normal. At this stage of the pandemic, no one knows what
the future will be like. I have finished writing this book under those circumstances. My purpose has not been altered by the uncertainty, lack of social
contacts, and anxiety caused by this deadly COVID-19 virus. It has been
impossible, though, to avoid being influenced by what it is doing to our lives.

My basic approach in this book, looking for God from below, from
where we are, now seems even more appropriate. God's immanence, more
now than before, outstrips his transcendence in importance. This does not
mean that God's transcendence is to be ignored, much less denied. But
Christian faith is about God with us, here and now, a down-to-earth God.
The Lord's Prayer is a case in point. It is about the realm of God being
known here on earth. This prayer speaks to the concerns of regular people,

and even more specifically to people who are not having it easy, such as the peasants in rural Galilee who were Jesus' usual audience, and we who are now facing a deadly virus. What those peasants needed was bread, the food for survival each day of their lives. And they needed relief from indebtedness, here and now. The Lord's Prayer is a prayer for this world, now. It is a down-to-earth prayer.

In much of history, life was difficult and short, with little comfort and no treatment for disease. At the age of eighty-eight, that is not how I would describe the life I have had. And, though we are experiencing an extreme division in our country, I do not think many Americans would describe their lives in pessimistic terms. Few of us would sacrifice life here for a life hereafter. Among the clergy, that is expressed by the saying: "Everyone in my church wants to go to heaven, but no one wants to go today." We can live only in the present, which is true not only of our life with family and friends, but also of our life with God. Life in God's presence is discovered and lived in our relationships with one another right now. It is in our relationships that we live and move and exist. Life, faith, and love are relational; God is relational.

The good news of the relation we can have with God began on the dusty roads of the Holy Land, down here. That good news is that God loves us despite our self-indulgence and offers himself to us as the gift of grace. He does this everywhere and always. As a gift, it need not be earned, and cannot be earned, only accepted. That acceptance, though, must result in more than correct beliefs or good behavior. It must become trust, trust in the God who is shown to us in the life of Jesus. What is shown by the life of Jesus is that we are invited into a relationship, defined by Jesus as a fine dinner party, or a great banquet. It is to be a joyful relationship with God, in the dynamic presence of the Spirit. It is to be a relationship that includes and enhances our relationships with one another. It is to be an unbroken relationship, an eternal relationship.

Christianity as life in relationships is so central to my beliefs that I have moved away from some of the more traditional explanation of the doctrines of the church. There are optional explanations, as I have found, that are more congruent with the scientific worldview of our time. Science is a questioning discipline, and theology is a search for the truth about ourselves and our God. Neither should be restricted by the other as we search for meaning and direction. In our search, struggling with what we don't believe is an important step toward finding out what we do believe.

SIDEBAR

My Prayer

LORD, KEEP ME IN the company of those who seek the truth, and, Oh Lord, protect me from those who believe they have found it. Amen.

Bibliography

Augustine. *City of God*. Translated by Henry Bettenson. Harmondsworth, Middlesex, England: Penguin, 1972.

Barclay, William. *The Gospel of John*. Vol. 1. Philadelphia: Westminster, 1975.

——. *The Gospel of Mark*. Louisville: Westminster John Knox, 2017.

Bass, Diana Butler. *Christianity after Religion*. New York: HarperOne, 2012.

Bellah, Robert, et al. *Habits of the Heart: Individualism and Commitment in American Life*. Berkeley: University of California Press, 1985.

Borg, Marcus J. *The Heart of Christianity*. San Francisco: HarperSanFrancisco, 2003.

Borg, Marcus J., and John Dominic Crossan. *The First Paul*. New York: HarperOne, 2009.

Brueggemann, Walter. *Introduction to the Old Testament*. Louisville: Westminster John Knox, 2003.

Capon, Robert Farrar. *Health, Money, and Love and Why We Don't Enjoy Them*. Grand Rapids: Eerdmans, 1990.

——. *Kingdom, Grace, Judgment*. Grand Rapids: Eerdmans, 2002.

——. *The Mystery of Christ and Why We Don't Get It*. Grand Rapids: Eerdmans, 1993.

——. *The Romance of the Word*. Grand Rapids: Eerdmans, 1995.

Cobb, John B., and David Ray Griffin. *Process Theology: An Introductory Exposition*. Philadelphia: Westminster, 1976.

Cross, F. L., and E. A. Livingston, eds. *The Oxford Dictionary of the Christian Church*. 2nd ed. New York: Oxford University Press, 1983.

Davis, Ellen F. *Getting Involved with God*. Cambridge: Cowley, 2001.

Dick, R. A. *The Ghost and Mrs. Muir*. Chicago: Ziff-Davis, 1945.

Dr. Seuss. *How the Grinch Stole Christmas*. New York: Random House, 1985.

Ehrman, Bart D. *The New Testament: A Historical Introduction to the Early Christian Writings*. New York: Oxford University Press, 2012.

Episcopal Church. *The Book of Common Prayer*. New York: Church Publishing, 1979.

——. *Hymnal 1982*. New York: Church Publishing, 1985.

Eusebius. *Ecclesiastical History*. Translated by Arthur Cushman McGiffert. Coppell, TX: Pantianos Classics, 2022.

Felton, David M., and Jeff Procter-Murphy. *Living the Questions: The Wisdom of Progressive Christianity*. New York: HarperOne, 2012.

Holmes, Urban T., III. *Turning to Christ: A Theology of Evangelization and Renewal*. Cambridge: Cowley, 1981.

Bibliography

Kant, Immanuel. *Groundwork for the Metaphysics of Morals.* Edited and translated by Allen W. Wood. New Haven: Yale University Press, 2002.

L'Engle, Madeleine. *A Swiftly Tilting Planet.* New York: Square Fish, 1978.

Lewis, C. S. *The Great Divorce.* San Francisco: HarperSanFrancisco, 2001.

MacCulloch, Diarmaid. *Christianity: The First Three Thousand Years.* New York: Penguin, 2011.

Macquarrie, John. *Principles of Christian Theology.* 2nd ed. New York: Charles Scribner's Sons, 1977.

Meyers, Robin R. *Saving Jesus from the Church.* New York: HarperOne, 2009.

Newell, J. Philip. *Listening to the Heartbeat of God.* Mahwah, NJ: Paulist,1997.

Norris, Richard A. *Understanding the Faith of the Church.* The Church's Teaching Series 4. New York: Seabury, 1979.

Pannenberg, Wolfhart. *Jesus—God and Man.* Philadelphia: Westminster, 1977.

Phillips, J. B . *Your God Is Too Small.* New York: Macmillan, 1961.

Seeliger, Wes. *Western Theology.* Houston: Pioneer Ventures, 1973.

Spong, John Shelby. *Resurrection.* San Francisco: HarperSanFancisco, 1995.

———. *Unbelievable.* New York: HarperOne, 2018.

———. *Why Christianity Must Change or Die.* San Francisco: HarperSanFrancisco, 1998.

Tillich, Paul. *The Courage to Be.* New Haven: Yale University Press, 2014.

Wright, N. T. *Simply Christian.* New York: HarperOne, 2006.

Subject Index

Abraham, 31
Abram, 6
absolute sense, of knowing, 111
Adam, 105–6
Adam and Eve, 24–25, 140
adonai, used instead of the name of God, 99
"Advocate," paraclete as, 135–36
affirmation of faith, Nicene Creed as, 63
agape, 102
Ahriman, 18
St. Alban, martyrdom of, 90
all-knowing, God as, 105–6
all-powerful, God as, 103–5
all-present, God as, 107–8
Amos, 124, 152
Animating Being, God as, 97
animation, image of, 96
Apocrypha, 30
Apostles' Creed, 76, 112–13
appeasement, 156
Arianism, 62, 112
Arness, James, 129
"ask, and you will receive," 154
asking favors of God, prayers as more than, 153
Athanasian Creed, 113
atheism, first Christians accused of, 87
at-one-ment, 75, 77
atonement, 75, 80, 81–83
attraction, mutual, 104
attributes, of God, 91, 101, 102–8

Augustine of Canterbury, 144
Augustine of Hippo, 95, 113, 115, 139–40
author of this book
    approach of, xvii–xviii
    excused from Sunday school, 5
    prayer of, 178
authority, 103–4
authors of the Bible, 32–33, 34, 41
Avatar movie, 159

"back to nature" theme, 4
bad things, 11, 108
baptism of Jesus, 125
Barclay, William, 133
Bass, Diana Butler, 157
behavior, using good, 3
belief, 3, 10
Bellah, Robert N., 151
Bible
    as about relationships, 6, 9, 29
    inerrancy of, 34, 45
    reading in three ways, 43–44
    as record of our response to God, 41
    role of, 173
    as several books, 29–30
    translations of, xvi
The Big Fisherman (Lloyd Douglas), 56
Blake, Amanda, 129
blame, shifting, 15, 24
blaspheming, against the Holy Spirit, 137–38
blood of Jesus, images of, 78

181

Subject Index

parables, 104, 170
   good Samaritan, 41, 104, 171
   late-night friend, 154
   loving father, 156
   nations, 9, 78–79, 115
   prodigal son, 40–41, 156, 170
   unjust judge, 154–55
   wedding feast for the king's son, 79
   wheat and the weeds, 21
parakletos, as reference to the Spirit, 135–36
participation, in the nature of Jesus, 61
The Passion of Christ movie, 76
Passover, instruction on, 94
Passover meal, Jesus' Last Supper, 33
pastors, of large prosperity gospel churches, 148
St. Patrick, 143–44
Paul
   bad rap from letters he probably did not write, 51
   explanations of the at-one-ment, 77
   on God as the universal giver of life and breath, 134
   on God's love towards us, 160
   inspiration of, 48
   on James as an apostle, 61
   on the nature of the resurrected body, 67
   on no condemnation for those united with Christ Jesus, 149
   on reconciliation, 8, 163
   on resurrection appearances, 68
   on sin coming into the world, 24
   on the Spirit of God dwelling in you, 127
   vocation of, 164
   working with God's presence in Jesus, 95
Pelagianism, 140
"penitence," 127
perseverance, of God's love, 102
Persian thought, as dualistic, 18
person, mystery of a, 92
personness, possession losing, 37
persons with us, as better than answers, 168

Peter, 32, 70, 125, 168
Pharisees, 15
philia, as social love, friendship, 102
physical resurrection, demanding an empty tomb, 73
plagues, God inflicting on the Egyptians, 94
plan
   of God for each of us, 108
   God not having for anyone, 131
poetry, Nicene Creed as, 63
Pontius Pilate, 62
possession, as dehumanizing control, 37
postmodern world, formed by various communities, 150
power, of the Spirit, 126
power struggle, in every marriage, 103
prayer, 153–54, 155, 178. *See also* Lord's Prayer
presence of God, 108, 165, 176
The Principles of Christian Theology (John Macquarrie), 91, 96
private spirituality, not possible, 139
process theology, 109–10
Procter-Murphy, Jeff, 92, 106–7
prodigal son, parable of, 40–41, 156, 170
prophets, 8, 123
prosperity gospel, 87–88, 148
providence of God, 131–33, 153
province of the Spirit, getting, 131
Psalms, 47, 92
public ministry, of Jesus, 57
punishment, 5, 78

Quirinius, governor of Syria, 45–46
Quo Vadis (Henryk Sienkiewicz), 56

ransom theory, of the atonement, 82
rapture, as unbiblical and mistaken, 97
reconciliation, 6, 8, 77, 78
Red Sea, escape of the Israelites through, xiv
Reformation, 21
relational situations, seeking God in, 107
relations, heaven and hell in terms of, 15
relationship with God, 23–24, 115, 161

Scripture Index

Scripture Index

Mark (*cont.*)

13:32 NEB	57
14:12 NEB	33
14:16–17 NRSV	45
14:26 NEB	33
14:33–34 NEB	58
14:54 NEB	70
14:70 NEB	70
14:71 NEB	32
15:24b NEB	158
16:1–8	73
16:7 NEB	74

Luke

	13, 14, 33, 38, 39, 40, 45, 46, 60, 66, 93, 124, 154
1:3 GN	52
1:35 NEB	125
2:1–20	39
2:2 NEB	45
3:22	134
3:23 NRSV	57
3:23–38	57
4:1–13	14
4:14 NEB	126
4:18–19 NEB	124
6:17a NRSV	40
6:20 NRSV	40
6:24 NRSV	40
6:36 NEB	93, 127
7:34b NEB	57
9:24 GN	176
9:28–36	69
9:58 NEB	87
10:18 NEB	13
10:25–28	173
10:29–37	41
10:29–37 NEB	104
10:30 NEB	171
10:33 NEB	171
11:4b NEB	154
11:10 NEB	154
11:13 NEB	154
12:10	137
15:11–32	40
15:20 NEB	156

18:2–8	170
18:5b NEB	155
19:1–9	174
23:49 NEB	70
24:1–11	73
24:30 NEB	66
24:30–31 NEB	66
24:31 NEB	66
24:39 NEB	66
24:41 NEB	67
24:50–51 NEB	43

John

	12, 14, 45, 46, 47, 60, 61, 65, 67, 74, 97, 135
1:1–5 NEB	60
1:1–5 RSV	47
1:1–18	60
1:2–5 KJV	96
1:2–5 NEB	96
1:2–5 NRSV	96
1:14 GN	60
1:18 NEB	170
1:29 NEB	33
1:32	134
1:32–33 GN	141
3:5 NEB	126
3:8 NEB	135
3:16	117
3:16 NEB	102, 117
5:17 NEB	12
6:15 NEB	14
6:30–31 NEB	14
7:3–4 NEB	14
7:5 NRSV	60
10:10 NEB	110
10:30 NEB	118
11:21–24 NEB	71
14:9b NEB	170
14:16	135
14:16 NEB	136
14:26	135
14:26 NRSV	135
15:5 NEB	95
15:26	135
15:26 KJV	135

Scripture Index

Made in the USA
Las Vegas, NV
13 July 2024

92270961R00132